SPINNING INTO CONTROL

HOW SURVIVORS INSPIRE YOUR SUCCESS

PATRICK T. FINLEY

Prodigy Press, LLC

This book is intended as a reference volume only. It is sold with the understanding that the publisher and the author are not engaged in rendering any professional services. The information given here is designed to help you make informed decisions. If you suspect that you have a problem that might require professional treatment or advice, you should seek competent help.

Published by Prodigy Press, LLC
Copyright © 2017 by Patrick Finley

Cover design by Sheila Parr
Book design and composition by Sheila Parr
Cover images © Makushin Alexey / Shutterstock,
Polushkina Svetlana / Shutterstock, GeorgePeters / iStock

ISBN: 978-0-9984180-0-1

Printed in the United States of America

First Edition

To Logan and Chase—my sons who I admire for your courage and perseverance in finding your way

To my wife, Gina—my granite, my undying advocate, my confidence when I had none

To Tom and Ellie—my giving and wise parents

Adversity is a horrible thing to waste.

—Captain Joseph Charles (Charlie) Plumb,
  US Navy, retired

CONTENTS

FOREWORD

Because his name might not yet be familiar to many of you, I'd like to introduce you to Wade Hoag before you read the foreword he so graciously contributed to this book. Wade's life-altering accident occurred while I was writing this book. He and I had long discussions about what it means to be a survivor; many of those took place while he was just starting to figure out his new life. His feedback and support were instrumental in helping me finish this book and fine-tune the REACH protocol you'll read about in its pages.

Wade is what I call a "Champion Survivor," a remarkable inspiration to me and to many others. Although his legs may not work, his sharp and creative mind sure does. I look up to him and thank him for all he has done and will continue to contribute to the many others struggling for perspective and meaning in their own survival.

The majority of us—7.4 billion people in the world—are surviving something everyday of our lives. From nine-to-five drudgery, disabilities, and divorce, to natural disasters, job loss, freak accidents, and cancer, we are all faced with things we cannot control, but have to face.

Survival is the common denominator of humanity. Survival

is what ties your story to Pat the businessman, Stefani the wife and mother, Louis Zamperini the war hero, and me the nineteen-year-old kid. (These are all people you will meet in this book.) Survival cuts through time. In many ways, our ability to survive makes us human, while in other ways it makes us animals, illuminating both our humanity and inhumanity.

Spinning into Control describes the full spectrum of survival, the melody we hum along to daily. The level on which this book speaks to you will depend on where life has taken you. I know *survival* meant something much different to me a year ago than it does today.

Had I come across this book before my accident, the stories would have entertained me. I would have taken note of Pat's advice. Then I would have thought about how REACH applied to whatever problem felt pressing at the moment. And that would have been a perfectly acceptable use of *Spinning into Control* and the protocol Pat describes. It would even have been good practice for whatever was to come down the road.

If you are someone who has yet to experience survival (and I mean survival), I expect that you will relate to the book much like I described above. Read *Spinning into Control* now. Keep Pat's voice in the back of your head. This book will continue to make sense long after you've put it back on the shelf.

If you are someone who has known true *survival*, this is a book you should read now. Pay close attention. Keep listening to the stories of those who have survived and replace their names with your own. I think you will find that elements of their stories are not too far from your experience. In one way or another we are all stranded at sea, bound to wheelchairs, or terminally ill. Life's storms are inescapable, but we continue on. We survive. "I can't go on. I'll go on." The words of Samuel Beckett are etched in the foreground of our struggle.

Survival is the most rattling, heartbreaking, painful, profound, and ultimately beautiful display of endurance. I have found that survival can be tragic, but it is not always a tragedy. Survival can be as peaceful as it is uncomfortable. Like death, like grief, survival can be both lonely and communal. The ability to balance those dichotomies, to choose which side of the scale you will sit on at any moment, is where you will find your ability to survive.

Mike Hoag (left) and Wade Hoag (right)

Survival, like most things, hinges on a series of choices. Life either means something . . . or it doesn't. And we decide that our life means something and go after it with some fury . . . or we don't. Pat has laid out clearly what it means to live in spite of what life has given you. He tells the understated and elegant story of survival and frames the question: What will you do with what has been done to you? What will you R.E.A.C.H. for?

Take the foundations of REACH and these stories to make discoveries on your own. *Spinning into Control* works for me—for anyone—because you will fill in the blanks and shape-shift the stories so that they speak to your own experiences.

It wasn't until I had gone through my initial catastrophe that I realized I had done everything Pat wrote about here. Certain stories that would have just been entertainment for me a year ago now strike a deep chord. Everyone's been through something, and some of those lessons help me frame my story in a different light. Especially the people who got through their "something" and managed to still have a meaningful life.

Find the meaning in survival, because survival never ends. Are survival and life mutually exclusive this book asks you. The answer I have found is that our ability to survive and our deep desire to live are one and the same. That's the answer that gives shape to long days when going on seems too much. I found it. I find it every morning. I hope you do too.

Wade R. Hoag
Fall 2016

PROLOGUE

SPINNING INTO CONTROL

September 3, 2010

The helicopter began to spin violently. My eyes blurred. The g-force slammed my body into the starboard side window, practically ripping the controls out of my sweaty hands. I desperately tried to keep a grip on the stick.

My adrenaline rush was so intense I felt like a basketball had lodged in my throat and chest. There was no breath, no air. In my foggy peripheral vision, I saw the altimeter dropping hastily. My passengers—both business partners of mine—and I were plummeting toward the earth and certain death. I was quickly succumbing to panic—and to the helicopter's mesmerizing uncontrolled spinning.

For a few surreal seconds it enticed me into giving up and letting the dreamlike ride take us where it wanted. Down and down.

Thankfully, that momentary passiveness was quickly shattered by the snap realization that we were going to die! But I had worked too hard in recent years, repairing my fractured life, to allow it to be destroyed *today*. We weren't going down without me using every bit of training and preparation I had to save us. I was in charge. I was responsible. Six seconds. Time to go!

I slammed the stick forward and downward, blasting us *toward* the highway on-ramp. I made the choice to trade precious time in order to regain a little control. Three seconds. The slanted concrete was coming. There was no way we'd make it out in one piece. My passengers gasped. Two seconds. Escaping the downwash, I pulled back on the stick like you would the reins of a runaway horse and heaved the helicopter back. It responded. Our swirling nosedive transitioned to a flat, stymied descent.

One second. The faded white lines on the highway came into frighteningly detailed focus. Here we go . . . here we go . . . BANG!

We were on the ground. *Alive!* The helicopter blades looked like waving noodles; the engine whined in distress.

We were on the ground, alive, but in the middle of a steeply graded highway on-ramp!

"Holy shit," yelled one of my passengers. I looked up. A semi-trailer truck was rounding the corner of the ramp and heading toward us. "Get out! Get away!" I yelled to them over my shoulder.

My passengers fled the wreck. The oncoming 18-wheeler slammed to a halt a few yards from my machine and me. Not thinking, not taking a moment to breathe, I urged the blades to spin faster. The engine sounded normal. I slowly and carefully eased the helicopter off the pavement. At least my passengers and I had escaped the notoriety of starring—posthumously—on the 6:00 o'clock news.

Fortunately our intended destination was only about a thousand feet further east. My passengers elected to walk. I couldn't blame them.

I guided the injured helicopter to a soft landing near the office we were supposed to be visiting, a big complex right off the highway flanked by wide green lawns. This was one of the buildings in our investment portfolio, and we regularly made on-site visits. Sometimes, because I have my helicopter license, I would fly us over. Never had I imagined . . .

I got out and began to survey the helicopter. Surely the damage was irreparable. Catastrophic. But, other than some slight crinkling near the mast, the aircraft was sitting on the grass as if nothing out of the ordinary had happened. It appeared to be flyable, and I was alive. Had it all been a dream?

Just then I noticed a stinging in my knee from where my leg had slammed into the instrument panel. And stiffness started to come on in my back. Okay, it wasn't a dream; it really *had* happened. I wasn't a hunk of metal and flesh on a Columbus freeway. I was alive. My hands began to shake as though I were in Arctic temperatures despite the warm morning sunshine. The crash was slowly sinking in, and all I wanted to do was escape from my own body. My passengers had immediately hoofed it into the office. I followed after them, desperate to get away from the chopper and try to calm down.

What next? How could I fix the mess I was now in? Ignore it? Sweep the crippled chopper under a very big rug? At that moment I wished I were anyone but me.

It seemed pointless to carry on with the site visit we had scheduled. I sent my passengers off in a car. I barely remember what they said, but I had the distinct impression they were grateful to get out of there. It'd be a miracle if they came near me, or a helicopter, ever again. I was on my own. Me and the injured bird.

I dialed my mechanic (despite knowing this would set off the chain of aviation gossip). He was about a hundred miles away and couldn't make it out at that moment. I asked him how to perform a visual inspection for symptoms that might indicate I had done damage to the engine, transmission, or blades. He gave me the rundown, and my confidence began to return. I felt like I had a plan.

As I was concluding my conversation with my mechanic, I saw lights flashing and heard sirens blaring outside. Mysterious unmarked black cars. Surrounding the helicopter that I had abandoned fifteen minutes earlier.

I approached one of the men who had gotten out of the car and was now staring at my chopper. He was looking anxious and sporting a badge I couldn't place. "May I help you?"

"We got word someone stole a helicopter and crashed it here. Then ran," he said.

It wasn't a dream; it was a nightmare. The adrenaline high I was already riding spiked again.

I tried to be nonchalant. "Doesn't look like a crash scene, does it? I'm the owner of the helicopter—and this is my land." One of those things was true.

A little sheepishly he admitted, "Well, I guess not . . ."

The badge. He wasn't police. Department of Homeland Security.

Oh, shit. Getting Homeland Security involved in this would make matters very complicated, causing an unwarranted hassle. I needed to slither my way out of there before he asked too many questions and this got ugly. I would have survived the crash only to die under mounds of paperwork.

"But what happened here?" he asked suspiciously.

I glibly came up with some answer about a false warning due to sunlight that resulted in my emergency landing. I sold it well.

"I see. No problem, sir. This location is within five miles of an international airport, so we're required to . . ."

I assured him it wasn't an issue. I was just about to move the helicopter anyway, I explained, so there was really nothing to see. The words came out of my mouth before I thought about what I was saying. Fly the chopper again?

"Do you mind if we stay and watch you take off?"

Now my fate was sealed.

For the second time that day, I climbed into my flying scrap-metal coffin. Before stepping in, I'd done the prescribed visual inspection and nothing looked amiss. I tried to make it look like it was normal to fly a helicopter that had nearly crashed just twenty minutes earlier. I plastered a jolly smile on my face. Wasn't this fun?

Once more my adrenaline kicked into high gear, erasing any semblance of critical thinking that existed in my brain. Any rational decision making that would have pointed to obvious solutions, such as "Go home and come back tomorrow *with the mechanic!*" I had lost my mind.

The engine started right up. The blades squeaked and wobbled to life. Hovering. Moving back and forth, side to side. Careful, slow, easy—what the *hell* was I doing?

I brought the helicopter up and over the trees that, minutes earlier, I was sure were going to be my final resting place. As I picked up more speed, my palms grew sweaty on the stick. Though the helicopter wasn't making the high-pitched whirring sound that had started about a minute before we fell like a stone toward the highway, I still didn't feel comfortable. My "smart" thought was to fly above those busy freeway lanes. If I was going to crash again, that grassy median looked like a good spot . . .

A slight bump occurred with every rotation. I prayed the helicopter was all right. (*All right?* Who was I kidding?) It was a borrowed bird, and I knew the owner wouldn't take kindly to the abuse. I was having trouble focusing. Sweat beads formed on my forehead. I started making deals with myself. Never again. Next time.

After what seemed like hours but was actually fifty minutes, I slowly approached the airport. The mechanics were waiting for me. I made the landing, and everyone looked relieved. My momentary triumph was shattered by the realization that there was going to be a price to pay. Was I better off dead or alive? My life was already in shambles. My family. My business. And now this helicopter.

As the helicopter shut down, my phone rang over and over again. The owner, informed by his mechanic, was calling to inquire. I came clean (well, softening the edges a bit). He took it well, getting off the phone to get hold of his attorney, the banks, the FAA, the law . . . I put my face in my hands. My embarrassment was complete.

Mechanics scoured the helicopter, noting the cosmetic damage to the cowling, the stress to the landing gear, and a crinkle in the main struts (ouch). I was proclaimed a lucky bastard.

At home, an hour later, my phone rang again. This time the mechanic's macho voice had been squeezed up several octaves.

"We pulled the helicopter into the hangar and got a ladder

to check out the blades. One blade was *completely cracked and severed. It was only attached by the Kevlar outer skin!*"

Somehow, 3,000 pounds attached to blades spinning at 300 mph didn't totally disintegrate the Kevlar. If that had happened, there's no emergency procedure in the world that could have saved me or my passengers. Death under any condition. The aircraft would have dissolved into a million pieces due to the excessive violent vibration midair, and I would have been left strapped to an unwrapped seat going over a hundred miles an hour.

But it didn't. I survived.

INTRODUCTION

September 3, 2010

My story didn't end on an on-ramp in Columbus, Ohio, among broken pieces of a helicopter. *I survived.*

To help you put my near-fatal accident in perspective, let me share what was so special about that date.

Exactly thirty days earlier, I had had my final day in court to end a three-year-long, heated divorce battle that—in addition to dismantling our family—had locked up my business and almost bankrupted me during one of the worst economic recessions in US history.

September third was the final day my ex-wife could appeal the divorce. I was supposed to be celebrating closing this ugly chapter and getting a chance to rebuild my life and the lives of my two teenage sons. Instead, in an ironic twist, those last three years of misery had almost ended abruptly and violently in a drama fit for the closing shots of a James Bond movie. I would have died a failure as a pilot, husband, father, and business partner.

Sitting in the passenger seat as a friend drove me home on that fateful day, my head was flooded with adrenaline-fueled mixed emotions like I've never felt before. I was elated to be alive. Yet, at the same time, a searing anger quickly overpowered the joy I felt at having survived and the appreciation of being spared. I was absolutely, unsparingly, unapologetically pissed at myself. Irrationally (the mechanical failure of the helicopter wasn't on my head, after all), I silently asked myself questions like, "How could I be such an idiot? How could I get myself into such a deplorable mess on top of all the other messes in my life?" My mind locked on the *how*, the *why*, the *what*, as in *what the hell am I going to do now?*

And then I realized: Those sixty seconds of controlled chaos in the helicopter had been like an ultra-condensed version of my struggle to survive in the previous three years. The same inflection points, the same decision-making strategies, the same path to survival. If I was going to make peace with any of this, I'd better start doing some real soul-searching.

What Makes a Survivor?

In the months that followed, I remained fixated on the questions Why did I survive? How was I so fortunate? Was it skill? Luck? Divine intervention? I started to study survival stories to try to understand whether my survival was a matter of luck, skill, or something else. I read countless books and articles and watched every interview I could find with all different kinds of survivors.

Centuries of literature and popular folklore are littered with stories of unlucky polar explorers, downed pilots, and stranded mountaineers. Everyone has a personal favorite story of epic survival, whether it's a shipwrecked castaway or pirate hostage.

Each of these stories celebrates the survivor at the heart of the narrative—and rightly so. These men and women are examples of humans overcoming immense adversity. But if you limit your focus to individual "extreme" stories of survival, you start to develop strange ideas about what it means to be a survivor. You get the impression that such survivors are superhumans forging unique paths to survival, that each scenario took a specific kind of thinking and skillset. You start to think the word "survivor" applies only to people who have lived through a plane crash or a hostage situation. You might even begin to believe that these extreme survivors are the exception, not the rule, when it comes to people's ability to be resilient.

But, if you consider survival more broadly—surviving illness, surviving the death of a loved one, surviving divorce—a different picture emerges. Survival in the context of this book includes the most trite of daily difficulties, the most infinitesimal of obstacles I apply survivorship to any challenge, any struggle, any bump that is eliminated using the same principles of perseverance.

I am lucky to count among my friends some truly resilient people. They have faced such dramatic survival situations as a traumatic brain injury, the death of a child, and cancer. Hearing about how someone dealt with Stage 4 Hodgkin's lymphoma or unexpectedly being confined to a wheelchair for life is a good way to put your problems in perspective.

Talking with these friends suggested to me that even extreme survivors aren't superhuman; they're ordinary people in bad situations who made smart choices. The problem with equating extreme survivors with superheroes is that we take away our ability to learn from the survival stories. Superman's problem-solving abilities aren't that helpful for me. But, if a man like Louis Zamperini is just another guy who, in crappy circumstances, figured out how to be phenomenally resilient, then I should be paying attention.

The more I researched and talked to people, the more I could trace the same elements, whether in stories about plane crashes, mountaineering accidents, or my own near-death experience. I found the exact same elements, five in all, in each survival narrative. While those five elements might go by different names or forms depending on the story, they were universal.

The Five Elements of Survival: REACH

I think about the five elements as a framework for survival. They're sequential, and meant to be adapted to your circumstances in whatever manner works for you. I am not here to tell you how to live your life—this is called REACH, not PREACH—but this is a framework that has held true for many people over centuries of human survival.

This formula is meant for both the moment of crisis, as when I found myself spinning downward in my malfunctioning helicopter, as well as the aftermath of the catastrophe. The short-term and the long-term of what it means to be a survivor. You can keep turning to REACH in every stage of your survival journey, looping the formula as needed.

Added up, the five elements result in a kind of tactical resilience that condenses into a handy acronym: REACH = Responsibility, Evaluation, Action, Confidence, and Happiness.

1. Survivors realize in the midst of the catastrophe that they must take *responsibility* for what has happened; they accept the role they had in creating the situation they are in, and they honor their obligation to survive.
2. Survivors spend energy on an *evaluation* of the situation by gathering information about the best way to proceed. Perhaps they consult wise people in their life or look to the

examples of other survivors. They analyze the information they have and create their own plan for survival.

3. Survivors take *action*, putting the plan they have created into effect. Sometimes this means aggressive action, sometimes this means strategic waiting. Regardless, they pursue their plan.

4. Survivors maintain full *confidence* in the plan they have created, showing an unwavering commitment to the decision they have made to survive.

5. Survivors find moments of *happiness* during the survival journey that buoy their faith in themselves and fuel their positive outlook.

In other words, *you* are responsible for your survival. *You* will create your escape plan. *You* must act on that plan and have confidence in that plan. And *you* need to find ways to stay hopeful.

I realize that my formula sounds a little simplistic. That's a good thing. When you are at a low point and tensions are running high, what you need is simplicity. Anything complex will go out the window because the situation itself will feel very muddied. You want a reflexive mantra—REACH—that you can pull out to center your attention on and start the business of surviving.

We Are All Survivors

Near-death experiences have a way of giving you a little clarity about what's important. Staring at piles of research and notes about survival and the magical "elements" that get people across the finish line, I wondered why I wasn't sharing. There was no saving me in the helicopter, but I wish someone had handed me a "Survival Handbook" during my three years of divorce trials and financial struggles. It might have made the journey up from rock bottom go a little more smoothly. I might have remembered sooner in the process to have hope, to make a plan, and to hold fast to the knowledge that there *is life after survival*.

I want to emphasize that I am *not* a survival expert. Nor do I want to be. I don't hold a PhD in psychology; I'm not a pastor; I'm not trying to sell you a service or convince you to join my cult. In my experience, people who purport themselves to be experts are often driven by an agenda or limited by dogma. This narrowness means that they get it wrong—quite often.

The benefit of coming at this with wide-open eyes is that I can be creative in my observations. In trying to map out what enables someone to succeed at survival, I didn't limit myself to psychological, physiological, or spiritual motivations. Educating myself from the ground up meant that I had to start with the fundamentals of survival.

Starting at the beginning also meant that I drew my conclusions not just from my own experience but also mostly from the experiences and insights of others. It was imperative that I listen with an open mind to what people had to tell me about their survival journeys—whether directly through interviewing them or indirectly in reading books and journal articles by or about them.

I was struck by one young man's story in particular as I was researching this book, a US Army veteran named Chris Mintz. The thirty-year-old decorated infantryman had the misfortune to show up for class at Umpqua Community College the day an active shooter rampaged through campus. As Chris tried to warn other innocent students, he was seriously wounded. His survivor's journey clearly exemplifies all five elements—responsibility, evaluation, action, confidence, happiness—in the

REACH formula. Chris so inspired me that I've chosen to open each of the book's core chapters with a scene from his journey as it unfolded.

REACH is more than just a handy acronym; it's a mindset. It isn't always intuitive. And you'll notice that the framework is relevant for more than just the big life-or-death survival moments. I use REACH in my daily life to address challenges ranging from solving business problems to tamping down road rage. In fact, the REACH protocol has become the framework of our company's culture. We triumph over our everyday problems and obstacles sometimes by strategically employing these principles multiple times a day.

REACH is a problem-solving mantra. The more you practice, the more reflexive it will become—so that you have the protocols at your fingertips before you find yourself in an emotional moment. Yes, this book is about moments of true survival, but REACH can be used as a way to *live your life*.

Beyond *Spinning into Control*

The final chapter in the book, "Writing Your Next Chapter," discusses life after survival. Your survival journey will most likely occur in several phases: the decisions you make in a split second, the near-term consequences of those decisions, and the long-term evolution of your survival story. The REACH protocol can be helpful not once but many times as you move through different stages of your long-term survival journey— whether you are living with a disability, healing from a broken relationship, or managing posttraumatic stress. For some, surviving is a process that never really ends. The strategies in this chapter will help you in the most long-term aspect of your survival journey, surviving survival.

What I've shared in this book forms a platform on which you can build your survival skills. It shouldn't be the end of your survival reading, however. At the back of this book you will find a "Survivor's Library" of resources that lists everything from the science of resilience to memoirs of Antarctic survival should you want to dig deeper. Some of the stories are hair-raising; all are uplifting. In reading about what others have accomplished, it is hard not to be inspired. Their survivor stories showcase the incredible strength, resourcefulness, endurance, and hope we humans are capable of.

What You Gain from Adversity

I am about to tell you, before we get in any deeper into *Spinning into Control*, that adversity has the potential to be one of the most positively powerful experiences of your life. Don't stop reading. I'm in no way minimizing the hellishness of survival. I just want to make it clear that you will walk away from your survival experience a better and stronger person, even if you can't possibly envision that for a long, long time.

You are going to read survival story after survival story in this book, including my own. I can only speak for myself, but, while I would never choose to go through what happened to me, I don't regret how my outlook on life has evolved precisely because of my survival experience. I would never change that or give it up, even if it comes with all the crap. The ugliest experiences I could ever have possibly come up with have brought some of the greatest joys to my life.

I think you will find that the survival experiences chronicled in this book are circumstances you would never wish on anyone. Yet, the survivors stuck in them transformed tragedies into moments that amplified character, created a crystal clear clarity of mind, enhanced relationships, and deepened their abilities to experience life.

Knowing this, I believe, makes it easier to commit to your survival. You don't have to believe me—when you're in the midst of survival, this positive outlook can feel unbearably cruel—but, someday, you will be able to count your blessings and your scars with a newfound perspective.

All the survival stories in this book are used as a metaphorical guide for all your own daily problem-solving challenges, large and small, trite and scary. The patterns are all the same. If you miss a step in applying the REACH protocol, your odds of solving the problem efficiently reduce dramatically. Memorize REACH, practice it, and make it part of your reflexive cognition. You will be amazed at what you can accomplish. You will raise your own bar for facing challenges, achieve more, appreciate more, and live a richer, more controlled life.

I stumbled on the REACH protocol by following my intuition . . . and then discovering, to my delight, that I wasn't unique in my story. Refer to this book whenever you are struggling. In times of chaos, it can remind you that you control more than you think, especially your mindset. As you work through surviving survival, return to the passages or testimonies that raised your spirits. And, if you see a friend or loved one struggling, yet you feel powerless to help, perhaps you can lend them this book along with your love and encouragement.

My wish is that, when you finish reading this book, you will be prepared to spin into control of your own life!

CHAPTER 1

RESPONSIBILITY

October 1, 2015. Chris Mintz was beginning his day of classes at Umpqua Community College near Roseburg, Oregon.[1] *The decorated US Army veteran, a North Carolina native, had resumed his studies as part of starting a new life in the Pacific Northwest with his wife and son. Today was his son's sixth birthday.*

Midway during his first class, Chris heard yelling, and then what was unmistakably gunfire. Chris and his teacher quickly evacuated the classroom. As he fled down the hallway, he heard someone say that no one had alerted the library. They would be caught by the shooter unawares.

Flee to safety and leave them to die or—

Chris ran to the library.

---

1 https://www.washingtonpost.com/news/post-nation/wp/2015/10/19/army-vet-hero-chris-mintz-opens-up-about-oregon-college-shooting/.

Sometimes disaster strikes you out of the blue, like a bolt of lightning from a clear sky. Other times you see the storm brewing long before the strike hits the ground. Maybe you were following proper lightning safety procedures, or maybe you were standing on a 14,000-foot mountain with a metal rod in your hand. However you came to be a victim, if you want to be a survivor, the first thing you must do is take *responsibility* for where you are right now and where you need to go. As Dr. Phil has said, "You choose your behavior. You choose your consequences."

Taking responsibility means assessing your circumstances. In other words, what are you responsible for? What is the situation you have found yourself in? What is on the line? What are the best and worst outcomes? What role, if any, did you have in creating this situation? Who is responsible for getting you out?

I want to make one thing clear before we dive in: taking responsibility isn't the same thing as blaming yourself. Forgiveness and responsibility go hand-in-hand in the REACH protocol. You can't move beyond step one if you don't forgive yourself for what has happened. No one is perfect, and survival journeys rarely go neatly. You won't always feel like the hero. Take responsibility for your choices, but don't dwell in shame.

The goal of this chapter is to help *you* become accountable, to take responsibility for your survival scenario. When things get ugly, survivors are the first ones to recognize the gravity of the situation and decide they have the tools to fix it. When you get stuck on the side of the mountain, you can't count on the chopper coming to get you. You will exponentially increase your chances of survival if you put yourself in charge of your rescue. It starts here. Give yourself the best shot you can at survival by taking the REACH framework to heart. And your first step in that process is to take responsibility.

I realize this advice—take responsibility—sounds so simple that it might be tempting to read quickly over this chapter. Don't. What sounds so easy in theory is incredibly difficult in the heat of the moment. Think about instances in your life when you delayed taking care of a problem. What were the consequences of that delay? While procrastinating about everyday decisions can create complications, delaying decisions in life-or-death situations can make the difference in your survival.

In this chapter you will learn how to overcome that fight-or-flight paralysis. You will also read about how to absorb responsibility for a survival situation that you've created or how not to get stuck in resentment if you had no hand in making the mess. Most importantly, you will spend time thinking about the *why* of survival—who and what do you fight for? Finally, this chapter will briefly touch on the role spirituality plays in survival.

The stories you will read in this chapter—suffering the death of a child, an accident that resulted in traumatic brain injuries, and near starvation after a plane crash—are about people who decided that their fate was in their own hands. They figured out what they could control and what they had to let go. My hope is that their journeys will inspire you to the same belief and help you take responsibility in your everyday struggles.

The Heart Pounds

Before you can take your first step in the REACH framework— namely, taking responsibility—there are three tendencies you need to realize that most people display when confronted with a survival situation. One is to deny the seriousness of the situation you are in or to deny there is a problem at all. The second is to recognize the disaster and to react like a deer in headlights: that is, freeze. The third is to look to someone else to solve your problems.

Falling victim to these responses does not make you a weak person. These three reactions are common and can be explained with a basic understanding of human physiology. In his excellent book *Deep Survival: Who Lives, Who Dies, and Why*, Laurence Gonzales goes to a lot of trouble to explain why humans faced with crashing planes or charging bears either insist that there is not a problem or decide to do nothing about it.[2] His explanation goes something like this.

As sentient beings with highly aware brains, we spend a lot of time gathering information about how the world around us works. We use that information to create predictive models of our lives. That sounds complicated, but all it means is that we make associations between scenarios and outcomes that allow us to function in our daily lives. For example, if I see rain clouds, I anticipate that water could come from the sky, so I grab an umbrella. If a dog is snarling at me, I don't pet it. Evolutionarily, this was handy for our Cro-Magnon ancestors as they learned to predict where they could find food or how to evade predators. Establishing mental models of the world was their key to survival.

In the modern world, however, our predictive brains have drawbacks. We build "models" of what we expect our world to look like and can have a hard time changing those models when pieces don't fit. For example, if we enjoy a local hiking trail and have hiked it a hundred times without seeing a rattlesnake, we establish a model for experiencing the trail that doesn't have

---

2   Laurence Gonzales, *Deep Survival* (New York: W.W. Norton & Company, 2004), 71–72.

snakes. Because we are not expecting a snake, if we *do* come across one, we react in one of two ways. We might not recognize the snake for what it is (we think it's a tree branch or a shadow) or we might not see it at all. On the other hand, we might see the snake and freeze, helpless against an impending strike. Our snake-free model has failed us.

Both responses have been well documented in studies and survival literature. A tragic example is the behavior of some people in the Twin Towers on September 11, 2001.[3] Despite feeling the impact of the planes and receiving evacuation instructions, many people continued to work at their desks. Others displayed a behavior not uncommon among victims of house fires or hurricanes: they began to slowly grab items they wanted to take along, even if it was something as nonsensical as a blank pad of paper. It wasn't about the utility of the items; their brains were just responding to extreme stress with a rote— and unhelpful—behavior.

These behaviors exist in everyday survival situations as well. How often do you see the parents of an adolescent son or daughter with a substance abuse problem seemingly blind to their child's increasingly dangerous behavior? And what about the young addicts themselves?

People facing grief, loss, or other issues often experience depression. This is normal. It's easy for lulls to become permanent or severe if steps aren't taken to halt your slide. I have seen people become stuck in paralysis and indecision until—eventually, inevitably—they are overcome by more serious issues. Making a decision to work yourself out of a place of indecision

---

3   Amanda Ripley, *The Unthinkable* (New York: Harmony Books, 2009), 8–10.

can come in many forms and might take more than just your own willpower. Working toward survival by using resources such as therapy or support groups is the very definition of taking responsibility.

That being said, it is understandable to resist positive encouragement or an uplifting mentality when you are in the early stages of mourning. Many times, the people around you want so desperately to do something to help get you to the other side. Their pushing, however, can have the opposite effect; you resist, especially if you are mourning. "Let me stay here in this horrible spot, because this is where I need to be. Leave me alone until I'm ready." This book and well-meaning friends are here when you are ready.

Beyond depression or grief, people "freeze" in their personal lives when a situation becomes overwhelming or intimidating. They cognitively *know*, for example, that they are undergoing a divorce or that they have created crippling credit card debt for themselves, but they can't seem to do anything about it. The activation energy to get going just isn't there.

When people stall out, they tend to look to others to either take responsibility . . . or to take the blame. I got stuck in my divorce when I blamed my ex-wife for the problems we were having. That was a dead-end road. It was on me to take responsibility. Remember: no matter what the situation is, it always comes back to you. You can't control what is happening to you, but you can control your response.

Putting yourself in the ring for the fight isn't easy. Moving past denial requires self-awareness and acceptance that your life, literally or figuratively, is on the line. Are *you* avoiding something? We all do, but hopping off that fence is imperative.

Sometimes the issue isn't freezing but figuring out where

rock bottom is. At times it's obvious. You're stranded on Everest with a storm coming in. Your boat has started to take on water. The divorce papers are in your hand. Whatever it is, the problem that needs solving is obvious and actionable. At other times, though, rock bottom—the moment when you know that your life is what you are fighting for—can catch you unaware.

When life gets hard, you owe it to yourself to stop and do a quick gut-check because of our human tendencies to downplay struggles until they hit a breaking point. Your intuition will tell you if there is a problem as long as you can be vulnerable enough to listen to yourself. Take responsibility. Ask yourself these crucial questions: "How serious is the situation I am in? What is the worst-case scenario that could result from this?" Survival requires that you repeat this mantra: *This **is** happening. What am **I** going to do about it?* Take it from one who knows. The helicopter **is** crashing, and you can't sit still, mesmerized by the uncontrolled spinning, any longer.

Life *Is* Unfair

It might be that you had no part in creating or contributing to your catastrophe. You happened to swim in the ocean the day a shark was spotted in the area, or you had the misfortune to be diagnosed with a serious illness. Alternatively, your survival situation might be a disaster entirely of your own making. (More on that issue in the section below called "We All Make Mistakes.") Either scenario requires a certain kind of mental fortitude to endure.

If you are a random victim of life's machinations, it can be easy to get angry. "Why me?"

As I was in the helicopter spinning perilously above the highway the day I was literally being handed my freedom, the irony was not lost on me. Why was this happening to *me*, such a qualified and conscientious pilot? And on the very day my life was being handed back to me. I started to get angry. But that was a mindset I had to quickly leave behind. Being mad would only cloud my thinking and waste time. No matter what, I was responsible for using my training and landing the helicopter safely.

Focusing on the injustice of the event and venting your anger is actually *not* a healthy way of processing life's ups and downs. Yes, something unfair has happened to you. If there is a loss associated, take time to mourn that loss. But there is no proven scientific benefit of taking a time for complaining. Actually, complaining makes us feel worse. Psychologist Jeffrey Lohr explains it (rather coarsely) this way: "People don't break wind in elevators more than they have to. Venting anger is similar to emotional farting in a closed area. It sounds like a good idea, but it's dead wrong."[4] I agree with him. Don't get mad; get productive.

Rick Doody lost his eighteen-year-old son to a tragic and senseless car accident (along with Alex's close friend Josh Weil). He confesses that dealing with the prevailing moments of extreme disappointment or sadness brought on by grief has been challenging. "It's not healthy to be overwhelmed by it all. The only alternative is to continuously strive to be as positive as you can even if you don't really feel like it."

The magnitude of the loss feels, understandably, enormous. "Alex and Josh were great young men loved by so many. They were kind and humble and good athletes in their respective

---

4 Jessica Stillman, "Complaining Is Terrible for You, According to Science." http://www.inc.com/jessica-stillman/complaining-rewires-your-brain-for-negativity-science-says.html.

sports. They were great students and friends and sons and broth-ers," Rick says, "It takes a lot of work, not giving into the grief. Sometimes you have to fake it to make it."

For Rick, the way to move past feeling ripped off by a life taken too soon is rooted in gratitude. "You have to find something to be grateful for—no matter what. When you are grieving, it's the last thing you want to do. But you have to look until you find it."

Rick's gratitude is rooted in two things: the meaningfulness of Alex and Josh's lives, and the loved ones he has around him. "Alex and Josh's death has touched so many and will inspire so many of their friends to live full meaningful lives. And, I have two incredible, beautiful daughters I love dearly, an amazing woman who loves me and I love, and I get to work with some really cool people who do amazing work."

Alex's passing has affected Rick in other ways as well. "I don't let the little things bother me anymore," he shares, "I see people getting upset about things so easily, and I just shake my head and think about how little they have to worry about and how much worse it really can be."

You heard from my friend Wade Hoag in the foreword to this book. Wade fell from a construction lift and is now confined to a wheelchair for life. (In chapter 6 he talks about how the REACH model characterizes how he's coped with surviving that loss.) He is nineteen. Nothing he did in his vibrant life merited the cards he was dealt, but he has to face his situation all the same. The cognitive dissonance that results from accepting that he is in a wheelchair while not accepting the implicit limitations of being in a wheelchair is the only way he can get up every morning. This mindset is his way of "accepting responsibility."

Fixating on unfairness is not an effective strategy for sur-vival; it will stop you from moving forward. You are right; what has happened to you is not fair. But here's a little tough love: no matter why or how this is happening, you are still accountable for your own survival and the survival of those who are dependent on you. (You'll read inspiring evidence of this in "Declare Your Dependents" later in the chapter.)

This isn't the time to focus on what you have lost or the hand life has dealt you. You can't afford to be angry. It takes some people a long time to get here, but the real progress starts when you can leave the anger and blaming behind. It's a process; don't expect to get into a healthy mindset all at once. One of the best ways I can illustrate that point is to share with you the story of my friends Roger and Stefani DePenti.

Stefani Schaefer is an award-winning top anchorwoman with FOX News in Cleveland, affectionately known by her maiden name to thousands of viewers. Roger DePenti decided to work for a successful solar company as a superintendent to learn more about the nuances of the business before he started a similar business of his own.

The happy couple had celebrated their twentieth wedding anniversary in Hawaii, bringing along their two children, Race (eleven) and Siena (nine), to show them where their parents had been married. On April 27, 2012 (just four months after that family vacation), Roger was up on some scaffolding helping his workmen install solar panels on a church when the boards gave way. Roger fell 12 feet to the ground. My wife, Gina, received the horrifying call from Stefani: "Roger is completely nonresponsive." He had suffered extreme head trauma and been airlifted to Cleveland's MetroHealth Level I Adult Trauma Center.

The DePenti family in Hawaii shortly before the accident.

Without warning or time to process what had happened, Stefani was rushed to his side and forced to immediately make critical medical decisions for Roger. (Though hesitant to do so, she nevertheless took responsibility, the first step in the REACH protocol.) The doctors could hardly mask their own stress as they encouraged Stefani to get the kids to the hospital to say a final goodbye to their father. I will never forget the look of disbelief on her face. Gina and I felt helpless to reassure her or give her hope. The situation was horrifying and surreal.

Roger had severe head fractures, brain bleeding, and brain bruising. He was in a coma and was put on a ventilator in the hope that he would miraculously stabilize and the complications would be minimized. Realistically, however, the doctors gave Roger less than a 10 percent chance of survival and warned that the brain damage would likely be devastating even if he did survive.

The first night in the hospital Stefani authorized the doctors to perform a craniectomy; part of his skull was removed to allow his brain to swell without damaging other cranial areas, particularly the brain stem. He survived the first battle. A day later, though, Roger began showing signs of an infection in his brain fluid. That shift from one critical situation to another would come to characterize life for the four DePentis in the never-ending freight train of complications that followed.

We All Make Mistakes

If choices you made are responsible for your disaster, it's a different story. Maybe you went skiing in whiteout conditions and then you couldn't find your way back to the lodge. Maybe you were part of an unhealthy relationship dynamic that you didn't attend to before it became destructive. Maybe you put off that doctor's appointment even though you knew something wasn't quite right.

Oftentimes your first reaction can be anger with yourself—"How could I be so dumb?"—or guilt. It's understandable. Knowing you are responsible for a situation that could end in your death or the end of life as you know it is unpalatable. But people make mistakes. (Recall that Alexander Pope said, "To err is human.") If you start reading extreme survival stories, you realize how frequently people make small misjudgments that put them in grave danger. The same is true in our everyday lives.

You *do* need to take responsibility for what you have done, especially if your choices have affected other people. Your mistake is a learning experience: don't forget it or repeat it. But in a survival scenario, your culpability is just another factor that needs to be acknowledged and incorporated. Recognize the mistake and then move on so that you can get down to the business of your survival. As I mentioned at the beginning of this chapter, this is where forgiveness is key.

Being mad at yourself is just precious energy wasted. This is true for the opposite scenario as well: If others are responsible for having put you in a bad situation, you have to forgive them. If you don't, the anger will be noise that distracts you from your survival journey.

Research has proven that forgiveness increases your psychological well-being: forgiveness makes you happier, less inclined to be negative, and even physically healthier.[5] If you can't get to a place of forgiveness at least try to set aside the resentment until you are out of the woods.

One of the survivors I interviewed for this book was US Air Force Colonel Leon F. "Lee" Ellis, retired. (You'll learn more about him in chapter 5, "Happiness.") Although he suffered horribly at the hands of his jailers at the Hanoi Hilton during the Vietnam War, Lee nevertheless miraculously and wonderfully believes in the power of forgiveness. "Forgiveness is usually grounded in love—and it starts with love for yourself." As he sees it, wasting his energy hating his captors or the Vietnam War agitators doesn't do him any good, so he doesn't engage with it.

Declare Your Dependents

Accepting responsibility for your survival is difficult. You have to decide that all the pain and crap you are going to go through in your quest to survive will be worth the life you have to live

---

5   Giacomo Bono, Michael E. McCullough, and Lindsey M. Root, "Forgiveness, Feeling Connected to Others, and Well-Being: Two Longitudinal Studies" University of Miami, 2007. http://www.psy.miami.edu/faculty/mmccullough/Papers/forgiveness_feeling_connected_pspb.pdf.

once the journey is over. That's what this book is really about: *Why* are you going to fight so hard? You must be able to answer this question.

Survival scenarios where nothing is certain, especially the finish line, are the most overwhelming. Taking responsibility for your survival when you can't see the road ahead is not a natural choice. Yet that's what a true survival situation is—not knowing the outcome when the stakes are your life. When the likelihood of survival is small and the pain is immense, it can seem easier not to try.

Sometimes the places your survival journey will take you are so dark that it is hard to imagine life being good again. It doesn't seem worth it to keep going for your own sake. It is in those moments that you must remember the people depending on you.

In my reading and interviews, in both extreme survival stories and the next-door variety, most survivors reported that they chose to keep going because someone was counting on them. At times this was a decision made for a loved one who was not part of the survival scenario but would be irrevocably impacted by the news of the person's death, like a parent or a child. In Chris Mintz's case, he knew that if he died on his son's birthday the family would forever associate what was supposed to be a day of celebration with grief. Yet, even if he was going to die, he preferred to confront the gunman and risk his life, because he envisioned his son remembering his father's bravery with great pride rather than sorrow.

Just two years ago, my friend Rick Doody (who I introduced earlier in the chapter) was presented with the opposite outcome: a father remembering his son's achievements with great pride rather than great sorrow. The events unfolded like this.

Alex and three of his close high school friends (Josh Weil,

Max Perlick, and Chapin Berk) were returning from lunch on a beautiful spring day. They were working on their final senior project at Alex's guesthouse, learning basic construction work like drywalling, painting, and minor plumbing and electrical.

Graduation was just around the corner for the boys. Alex was the captain of the Hawken basketball team and had hopes to play at Cornell where he was attending university the next year. Josh was captain of the football and lacrosse teams and was planning on playing lacrosse at Middlebury College. Max and Chapin played soccer at Hawken.

Alex had a slight concussion from a lacrosse game a couple of days earlier, so he let his friend Chapin drive the familiar route back to his house so they could get back to work on their senior project. It wasn't far. It was a beautiful day and the boys were feeling great about their college choices and their remaining days at Hawken.

The lightly traveled, hundred-year-old County Line Road tempted its invincible young driver into pushing the limits. An acceleration, then the roller-coaster terrain separated wheels from asphalt as the inexperienced driver fought for control—now sliding sideways off the berm, the passenger side of the car careening through wet spring grass, meeting an abrupt end against one of the many century-old oak trees.

Rick was on his way to a meeting at one of his restaurants when he got the call from the boys' construction superintendent that there had been an accident—and it was "real bad."

Rick kept asking, "How bad?"

"Bad . . ." was the response.

"Where is he?"

"On the way to the hospital."

He called his ex-wife Tammy and said he was really

scared—the boys had been in an accident. She asked if he could pick her up. When he went to turn onto County Line Road to get her, the road had been closed. He yelled to the police officer that it was his son in the accident, so the officer let him through.

When he arrived at his old driveway and looked north on County Line, all he could see were ambulances, fire trucks, and police cars. He picked up Tammy and sped off to the hospital, passing an ambulance and a biker who gave him the finger as he flew by. "I just kept shaking," he said, "I knew it was bad, and I was so scared."

When they got to the waiting room and asked to see their son, they were told to take a seat.

Several minutes later, which seemed like an eternity, an orderly called the two parents by last name and led them to an empty, generic waiting room just outside the ER. The Cleveland Clinic Hillcrest was in chaos, everyone scrambling to attend to the four boys who were being brought in one by one.

Rick and Alex's mother sat—and waited. Time began to slow . . . then stop. Something wasn't right. What was going on? Why weren't they being taken to Alex? They waited . . . and waited . . . and waited.

An abrupt knock. A harried doctor rushed in, not making eye contact. He turned to Rick and ushered him out into the hallway away from Alex's mother and said, "One of the boys is dead. You come with me." The stress made him cold, dispassionate.

Rick followed him down the long hallway and into an ER room. The room was divided by a curtain with at least a dozen doctors working on the boy on one side of the curtain and no one working on the young man on the other. A lonely gurney, and on it lay a body, still, clunky intubation tube blocking and distorting its facial features. Rick's myopic view began to widen as adrenaline pumped into his senses.

"Is that your son?" the doctor demanded, pointing to the body.

Rick couldn't process what he was saying. The limp body on the table? The images relayed from his eyes didn't make sense in his brain.

"Is that your son?" The doctor's tone had risen, barking the question over Rick's shoulder. The doctor held the chart out. It didn't have a name.

"Yes," Rick could barely manage, feeling as if he had disconnected with reality.

Rick describes how he felt walking away from that room. "Alex was gone. My son, my pride and joy, the boy I lived my life vicariously through, was gone. I walked out of the room and told Michael Weil, whose son Josh was being rushed off to surgery (where he would later pass on), that Alex is dead. Alone and in shock, I meandered back down the long, sterile and cold hallway. I had to go tell Alex's mother that he was dead. She screamed and together we cried. We sat in that room by ourselves in shock."

It was many months before Rick could begin to describe Alex's passing, how it affected him and how he managed to keep going. He needed time to grieve, as well as time to understand how sharing the experience would be meaningful. "I only want to talk about this if maybe someone else can be helped from my experience. If someone had told me that my son was going to be killed when he was eighteen years old, I would have said my life was over. But, somehow my life continues. When people ask me how, I tell them about this quote I found: 'You never know how strong you are, until being strong is your only choice.'" (Bob Marley)

Rick is a recovering alcoholic and celebrated twenty-five years of sobriety ten days after Alex died. He is active in the local AA community. "I would have been worried about falling back into drinking, but I still have much to live for," he says. For him, finding the purpose of his life is obvious. "I do it because I have two daughters I love more than anything, and a woman I love, great people I get to work with, and many, many friends whom I live for. I take responsibility for moving ahead for them."

Rick vacillates between feeling extremely sad and "ripped off" about Alex's loss and feeling so grateful for his two daughters, Sarah and Charlotte. The youngest, Charlotte, is attending Cornell this year, the school where Alex would now be a freshman on the basketball team. Wandering the campus with Charlotte for her orientation visit was extremely difficult. He had made the same walk a year ago with Alex.

Rick takes responsibility for working hard every day to uphold Alex's legacy, to cherish his daughters, and to proactively and consciously enjoy his friends and family—all the while struggling to accept this uninvited tragedy. Instead of succumbing to the tragedy, he fiercely fights for rich meaning.

He and the Weils have set up a foundation for the boys named Catch Meaning. On May 23 of 2016, just a year past the boy's death, the Doodys and the Weils hosted a Catch Meaning festival where thousands of kids came to support the boy's legacy and celebrate their lives while listening to some of their favorite music. The festival was meant to inspire kids to live full, healthy lives. As part of his therapy and the continuance of Alex's legacy, Rick was actively involved in promoting and selling tickets for the event.

One of his best sources of support in this tragedy has been Josh's father, Michael Weil. The two of them have the misfortune to share an experience that not many people can relate to: the loss of a son.

For many of us, the passing of a child would be our worst nightmare materialized. How could you go on? Rick has found a way.

In other cases, that sense of responsibility for others can even be for people who are not alive. Nando Parrado was a survivor of the famous Uruguayan Air Force Flight 571 plane crash in the Andes on October 13, 1972. The plane was carrying members of a Uruguayan rugby team, and of the original forty-five passengers, only sixteen survived the ordeal. Some died immediately from the impact of the crash; others perished later from injuries, exposure, and starvation.

I had the pleasure of hosting him for a couple of days as he was preparing to give a talk to my local chapter of the Young Presidents' Organization (YPO). Hearing about his experiences created a lasting impression on me. Moreover, his demeanor, confidence, and poise struck me as something I needed and wanted to learn more about. I found Nando to be the most pleasant, altruistic, and confident person I had ever met. He was so comfortable with himself; he radiated serenity, which made him very charismatic and easy to be around.

In his memoir, *Miracle in the Andes* (which was also made into a major motion picture), Nando writes that as he was stranded on the side of the mountain in the midst of the wreckage facing what felt like certain death, he decided he needed to put his life in order to honor the victims of the crash.[6] If he did

---

6   Nando Parrado, *Miracle in the Andes* (New York: Broadway Books, 2007).

not live there would be no one to tell their story. Nando also felt responsible for his father back home. His mother and sister had perished in the crash, and Nando knew that he was now all his father had left.

The author (right) with Nando Parrado.

He hunkered down for seventy-two days on the mountain before deciding that no one was coming to their rescue. Nando and another crash survivor, Roberto Canessa, spent the next ten days—through sheer determination and bravery—trekking through the Andes before finding someone who could alert the authorities and create a rescue mission to bring back the other survivors. As he was struggling out of the mountains, Nando explained to me: "I couldn't speak because my body was consuming itself to survive, and my esophagus was being eaten by my stomach acids. I thought of my father alone and pushed for another step."

Similarly, thoughts of being reunited with his wife motivated acclaimed author, psychologist, and Holocaust survivor Viktor Frankl. In 1942, Viktor and his immediate family (including his new wife) were moved to the Theresesienstadt concentration camp, where they would remain for several years until Viktor was sent to an offshoot of Dachau and his wife to Bergen-Belsen. Viktor witnessed unspeakable atrocities during this time and was pushed past the accepted limits of human resilience. His survival came down to the hope that he would see his wife again and finish the manuscript that he fervently wished to see published.

Of the two dreams, only one was realized. In 1945, Viktor was liberated from the camps but he discovered that his wife had been killed at Bergen-Belsen. He finished his book *Man's Search for Meaning*, which describes his experiences as a prisoner in the camps while also examining the experience from a psychologist's viewpoint. He notes that there was a fundamental difference between those who survived life in the concentration camps and those who didn't: the people who made it had something or someone to live for. For Viktor, it was his wife and his book. For others, it was a child or a friend.

I think his observation is still true today. All survivors have someone or something they are fighting for. For me, it was my girlfriend (now wife) Gina and my sons. If you don't feel like you have something worth fighting for, then it becomes your responsibility to create that meaning. The people who don't make it are the ones who have no purpose.

People who have no purpose often fall victim to behaviors

like alcoholism, inertia, or extremism. Purpose is fundamental to survival. It's not enough to want to survive; you have to know *why* surviving is so important to you. While we are hardwired for survival, when the darkest moments come, you will need the extra motivation that purpose gives you to get up and keep trying. Know the value of your life beyond what you can accomplish for yourself. Who depends on you? Who needs you? Who loves you? Who else loses if you can't live a full and purpose-driven life?

Your Spiritual Framework

In almost every survival journey discussed in this book, there is a spiritual element to the journey. For some people, this is founded in traditional religion. For others, it's a much less rigid spiritual "responsibility to survive."

This book is meant to give you a framework for survival that you fill in with your own beliefs and motivations. I am not here to provide answers to anyone's questions about a higher power or salvation. In that spirit, whatever spiritual mantra you choose (or don't choose) can be adapted to the REACH protocol. My one caution to you is that placing your fate in the hands of a higher power or luck doesn't absolve you from a responsibility to be vigilant about your survival. There's no free ticket, so to speak.

I grew up in an extremely Christian region of the country where I heard this saying a lot: Give your problems to God. That's not a bad stance, but I found that sometimes people used it as an excuse to stop taking responsibility for their problems. This is not a good strategy. Giving your problems to your higher power doesn't absolve you of the responsibility to actively solve your problems.

I once heard a parable that went like this:

There was a devout man who lived in a region prone to flooding. A horrible storm had been forecast to hit his town, and an evacuation order was given. Instead of evacuating, the man decided he would stay put. God would take care of him.

His neighbors drove by his house, begging him to come with them. There was room in their car. "I'm staying here," the man said, trusting that God would take care of him.

The flooding started, quickly filling the street and then rising to his doorstep. Soon his house was flooded.

A police boat came through. "Come with us," urged the policeman. "The water will only rise higher."

Again the man declined. "I'm fine," he said. "Help someone who really needs it."

Soon the man was forced to climb onto his roof. A rescue helicopter flew overhead and he heard over the loudspeaker someone shouting, "We're throwing down a ladder! Climb on and we'll take you away!"

The man shook his head and waved them off. God would save him, he thought, if he really needed help.

The flooding got worse and worse. The man's home was swept away, and he perished.

As he stood at the pearly gates, he scolded God. "Why didn't you save me?"

"I tried," said God. "I sent you a warning. I sent your

neighbors. I sent the police boat. And I sent the helicopter.
What more did you want?"

Whatever religion or belief you are calling on, remember that you are in the fight too. Spirituality is meant to buoy and empower you when things get ugly, but you must still show up.

When the bomb goes off, literally or figuratively, you will not be thinking clearly. It is human nature to minimize the problem, deny the problem, or look for someone else to solve the problem for you. But every minute you spend in denial or being ticked off at the world or yourself for putting you in this situation, you lose precious time and energy that could be spent on surviving the trauma.

You are responsible for the turnaround. Accept what has happened and decide that you can fix it. Forgive yourself for your mistakes. Remember what you are surviving for: yourself, a loved one, a better life, or some important unfinished business. If you know why you have to keep going, taking that first step is infinitely easier.

Make your survival journey about more than just your own outcome. Maybe it's a cause (telling the stories of those who perished) or a person (a child, parent, or partner—even a pet). Your life will take on a greater importance. You will find the strength to keep getting up even when you most want to quit.

CHAPTER 2

EVALUATION

Chris ran through the library, screaming at people to get out. And then he ran back to the classrooms where there were still people trapped inside.

In the first classroom he came to, he found a young woman covered in blood and sobbing. He knelt down by her, motioning for her to be quiet. Through the glass panel of the classroom door, Chris locked eyes with a student hiding outside, crouched behind a car. Chris waved at him to stay down.

The fellow started yelling at Chris to leave; he would surely be shot if he stayed inside with the wounded coed.

That Chris wouldn't do, but there was still one option for them.

"You need to go get the cops!" Chris yelled. "Tell them where we're at!"

Just then, the shooter turned the corner and headed toward the classroom.

In survival situations, the hardest thing to do is to think clearly. Confusion will be your biggest hurdle. You need to be able to think rationally in order to assess the situation you are in and to create a sound plan for survival.

This chapter begins with a quick explanation of how fear and stress affect the brain so you can understand what you are dealing with psychologically. I will discuss several techniques to help you calm yourself before making your plan, from simply taking a breath to deciding on explicit priorities. We will also talk about "Survival Profiles," or how to assess some of your innate qualities and behaviors that could help or hinder your survival before you get in a tough situation. And to complement and supplement what you bring to the table, I discuss the value of training and preparedness as well as giving your work ethic a checkup.

This chapter will help you build a survivor profile for yourself so you can begin to understand what some of your more and less helpful tendencies might be. Next we will focus on building out your support team, what I call your "Survival Cabinet," filling it with people and resources that offer possible solutions to the situation you are working to survive. Finally, we will discuss putting together your plan given your time and resource constraints.

The stories in this chapter are about plane crashes, permanent brain damage, mountain climbing accidents, a wildfire, and terminal illness, but ultimately, about people who understood that no man is an island. The most capable, tough survivors rely on others to help them through their survival journeys. When faced with a tough situation, these survivors tapped all their best resources of survival wisdom, including their own knowledge. They fought off panic, evaluated the situation from multiple perspectives, and came up with a plan that saved their lives or livelihoods.

Clear Your Mind

Being able to think rationally in life-or-death scenarios is key to survival. The more you can get your mental workings in order, the higher your chances of making it to the other side. Unfortunately, you will be working against your biology to do so.

When bad things happen, we become fearful or stressed—or both. The problem is that fear and stress chemically change the brain in ways that don't help us. The exact science of how stress changes the brain is beyond the scope of this book. (For a full rundown, read *Deep Survival: Who Lives, Who Dies, and Why* by Laurence Gonzales.) A simplified explanation is that stress releases cortisol and other hormones into your body, dramatically limiting the part of your brain that controls your complex thinking and planning. Where you normally might be able to evaluate multiple inputs and decide the best course of action, suddenly you find yourself stunned or on the verge of panic.

The effects of extreme stress cannot be overstated. Enough of it and your brain becomes so incapacitated that not only is complex decision-making difficult, you also start being unable to process what is going on. You are literally unable to see or hear what is happening around you.

During flight training in unrehearsed emergencies, I have experienced the inability to read simple instruments or words on an emergency checklist sitting right in front of my eyes. My vision shut down while my brain was trying to save me, too stressed by my impending doom. (This may be what people mean when they say they had "tunnel vision.")

Once you are in this limited state of mind, making rational decisions is almost impossible. Your logical mind is inoperable, and your emotions take hold. You will revert to basic emotional responses based on past experience—or just your emotions themselves.

If you have trained your instinctual emotional response in the correct way, you might be in the clear. For example, if you have taken defensive driving classes, the chance of you reacting correctly to prevent accidents is higher. If you have not, your emotions will dictate the outcome. You could be pushed into a fight or flight-type response.

When your brain enters a hyper-stressed state, you might not even be aware how impacted your thought processes have become. Asking a stressed person if he is able to make solid decisions is like asking an intoxicated person to assess his level of sobriety. No matter how well you think you are performing, it is critical that you take a moment to calm yourself or "sober up." If the survival situation calls for a split-second reaction, you will not have this luxury. But, even if you have five seconds before your helicopter goes into an uncontrolled spin, this is enough time to get your mental workings right.

Acknowledge that you are operating from a place of stress, which means you are not at optimal decision-making capacity. Be careful of knee-jerk reactions with a singular focus, which often come from experiencing tunnel vision. This is an impulse often seen in pilots in emergency situations where the aircraft is losing altitude rapidly. Unfortunately, it is a deadly one.

On June 1, 2009, the pilots of Air France Flight 447 from Rio de Janeiro to Paris flew into a storm and executed this very maneuver. Reacting to turbulence and the loss of speed indication, the co-pilot panicked and sharply pulled up the nose of the plane, stalling the Airbus 330. Instead of putting the nose of the plane down to gain speed and break the stall, as all pilots are trained to do, the pilots took no corrective action, continuing to try to fly the plane "up" while dramatically losing altitude. The plane fell continuously for five minutes and slammed into the ocean. All 228 people onboard perished in the incident.[7]

DON'T Trust Your Gut

A common piece of survival advice is "going with your gut" or "trusting your gut instinct." I want to address this quickly at this point in the chapter, because I am going to explicitly tell you the exact opposite: that is, be skeptical of your gut reactions. And I know some people will take issue with this advice.

In survival situations, a good plan or the right next step is usually not obvious. Because everything is so muddied, people often choose to rely on their intuition to guide them in moving forward. This isn't always bad. Your intuition can be a powerful tool. For example, I often see business deals where all factors point to success, but something just doesn't feel right to me. In these cases, I don't do the deal, and every time something happens down the road that proves my instinct right.

Is this because I'm prescient? Or do I have enough experience behind me that I no longer have to do painstaking quantitative analysis to determine whether or not a deal is going to work, and I'm able to "see" the deal for what it is? My guess: probably the latter.

My father actually doesn't believe there is such a thing as "gut instinct." In his mind, those two words are just a name for the subconscious thought processes we develop from training our brains to think a certain way. In other words, you can *train*

---

7   Jeff Wise, "What Really Happened Aboard Air France 447," *Popular Mechanics.*

your gut instinct to work for you. I would say that this means there is a big difference between making a "gut decision" with wisdom and experience (training) versus making a "gut decision" with no prior foundation as if you're sitting at the roulette table.

If you're in a situation where you feel like you need to go with your gut, ask yourself if you're starting blind or if you have some relevant experience here that could help guide you. If the answer is no, perhaps take a little time to question where your gut is leading you.

Running that analytical process in the foreground (*evaluation*) isn't a bad thing. In survival situations, you want to stop and evaluate your gut reaction. Said another way, evaluation is the cost of admission to survival in high-risk situations.

I could never solely rely on intuition when flying an airplane, for example. Flying at night or over the ocean without reference points, you can easily find yourself flying the plane at a downward angle and never notice (until you crash) because it doesn't *feel* like you're losing altitude. In those cases, you've always got to keep an eye on your instruments because your gut, intuition, emotional reaction will lead you astray.

This is exactly what happened to John F. Kennedy Jr. when he perished in an airplane crash on his way to Martha's Vineyard in 1999. He was not instrument rated, meaning he could fly in only clear conditions when he could easily make out the horizon and his plane's orientation relative to the ground.

His final flight was conducted in the dark, over the ocean, in hazy summertime conditions, making it very difficult to see where the horizon was located. I can attest that night flying over water without the sparkling city lights that pilots commonly see below them from the cockpit leaves you with a three-dimensional black void above, below, and beside the plane.

The crash reports cites JFK Jr. hitting the water at 270 knots in a plane that has a max cruise speed of 190. Given that no distress call was placed, he probably never knew he was crashing. The FAA report cites "spatial disorientation" as the pilot error responsible for the crash.

Unduly blaming JFK Jr. is not my intent in citing this example. Rather, his crash is a solemn reminder that even the most powerful and privileged among us aren't infallible. Be very careful of trusting your gut, especially if you're mixing overconfidence with risky activities and taking others along for the ride. You need your own set of instruments to help you be objective about forming plans when your emotions are sending you in the wrong direction.

The one case where you can let your gut instinct be the deciding factor is as it relates to "no go" decisions, like the business deals I describe above. If something seems too good to be true, or if something just feels off about a situation, trust your gut.

Otherwise, do yourself a favor and carefully consider your decisions. I know this seems counterintuitive when you're in an unfamiliar situation and it feels like all you have is your instincts to guide you. But you don't! You always have knowledge and experiences built up in your brain that can help.

Survival situations push people to the edge. You will find yourself emotional and very stressed. Working off of your gut reactions as a guiding force under those circumstances is a dangerous mode of operation.

Breathe; Prioritize; Keep Breathing

If you have more than a few seconds before disaster strikes, the first thing you should do is actively work to calm yourself before making any decisions. Try breathing exercises (counting breaths in and out). If you are a student of a practice like meditation, this is a perfect time to break it out. Some people might turn to prayer or secular self-talk, depending on their spiritual orientation. Anything that stops the free-fall into panic and starts helping your brain come to terms with your situation piece-by-piece.

I can relate to that loss of control. I remember every day that I had to head to the courthouse during my divorce proceedings. I would get in the elevator and ride it up to the third floor where the Family Court was located. The elevator doors would open and . . . instant panic. The air would just get sucked out of my lungs.

I had a two-step protocol I would follow when this happened: I would acknowledge this was a horrible place. A lot of people lost important things, like their marriage or custody of their kids, on this floor. But then I would remind myself that this was the first step. As long as I kept taking steps, someday it would get better.

Time and time again, when I find myself overwhelmed, the absence of a plan leads to panic. Sometimes the trick is to have a plan that requires no thinking. In aviation, for example, we have emergency plans so drilled into us that I probably recite them in my sleep. My hope is that REACH can be your go-to emergency plan. Practice it enough in low-risk but frustrating situations when you find yourself beginning to get overwhelmed so that when you are in a situation that inspires true panic your "training" will kick in.

If the survival situation you are in is long-term, like chronic illness, disability, addiction, or even the death of a loved one, you will have a different set of challenges. You will need to sustain your decision-making abilities over an extended period of time.

This can be difficult as you become fatigued. A key component of your success will be remaining positive (discussed in detail in chapter 5, "Happiness"), but you should also work to create an environment with as few stressors as possible. Your survival is your number one priority. Take care of yourself, but limit the rest of what you are trying to accomplish by excluding anything that does not directly relate to your survival outcome. Remember, noise distracts from survival.

You can't make these judgments unless you take the time to calm yourself and logically examine your motives. People under stress are not inherently rational, so the prerequisite for creating your survival plan is to put yourself into the kind of mindset that allows you to make the best decisions you can. Calm, controlled, and logical.

Nowhere have I seen this so poignantly played out as in the ongoing struggle of Stefani Schaefer and her two children. (You met the DePenti family in chapter 1.)

The first few weeks after Roger suffered traumatic brain injury, Stefani found herself living in a nightmare. She took emergency leave from work so she could be with him full-time. But she had to return to the studio all too soon. A cycle formed. She would wake up early in the morning, see the children off to school, head downtown to the studio, anchor the morning news, drive straight to the hospital, spend the afternoon there with Roger, go pick up her kids, run them to their activities, and then head back to the hospital at night.

Her weekends were spent at the hospital, Race and Siena in tow. She was mother, father, and caretaker, living moment-to-moment and hoping desperately for signs of improvement in Roger. "I thought me being there and helping with the therapies and trying to get through to him was going to help with the brain injury and bring him back to us," Stefani shared. "I was always the person who could fix something, but over many, many months I was beginning to realize that there was no way I could fix this."

Despite her total commitment and best effort, the situation was becoming unbearable. She was exhausted. The breaking point came one night on the way back from the hospital. After weeks and weeks of constant anguish and mixed messages, her eleven-year-old son broke down and told her how much he hated their life and what had happened to them. He said he wanted to die and begged for God to let him go. The pain was too much for Race to bear. He just wanted to escape any way he could.

That was the moment Stefani knew she had to take full responsibility and make some hard choices instead of continuing to throw herself solely into Roger's care.

> *The kids and I sat in that car for hours. I said, "There are mornings I wake up and wish I had not. The easy thing to do is give up and die. But Dad would never want that. He would want us to live—like he lived. No one in the world loved life more than your father and we have to show him that we are living . . . for ourselves and for him. The three of us aren't leaving this parking lot. It's good that we are talking about this, because we need to get a plan together—tonight. I'm not going to drive this car until we all have a pact. We decide whether we let this destroy us or define us, but we can't continue this way."*

Sitting in the front seat together, holding each other and crying, the three agreed that Roger would want them to live—and with purpose. He would want them to smile and laugh. That was how he had lived his life every moment he could. This was the moment she made her choice. She couldn't be all things to all people. It was time for her to limit her responsibility to what she could actually affect.

Stefani realized that putting her energy into "fixing" Roger was hurting her and her children. While he was out of immediate medical danger, Roger's injuries had devastated both his short- and his long-term memory. To her extreme disappointment and sorrow, he did not recognize either her or his kids. He could talk and even remember numbers, but he would quickly tail off into meaningless jumbled conversation. Nothing she did could make him better.

"Something doesn't go your way, you make it so it goes your way. I was that person, that wife, that mother. And then this was the first thing in my hands I couldn't fix. But what I needed to fix and focus on was what I had in front of me, which was our children."

Her family and friends supported her in this. Roger's mother was brutally honest, even telling her, "He doesn't know you and doesn't know if you are there or you aren't, but the kids do notice."

Stefani started to slowly adapt to their new reality. For example, when she first went back to work she had difficulty not just breaking down on air. She realized that coming into work wearing her pain so plainly was not sustainable. It also wasn't fair to her viewers. "I can't go to work and anchor a morning show and have people look to wake up and be happy, and then see someone sad, miserable, and aching. I can't do that to the viewers that supported me and prayed for us. I also couldn't do that to my coworkers. I had become such a sad, pathetic person.

I owed it to my coworkers to try to get back to the upbeat and positive person that I have always been. I needed to almost fake it. Smile. Pretend to be happy."

Opening up about her story also helped. She describes the support from her friends, family, and the community as being key, with boxes of letters coming in from people who had her family in their thoughts and prayers. Even small gestures had deep impact. One night Gina and I came over with pizza and a bottle of wine and forced her to sit and enjoy it with us. Stefani says, "I remember thinking, 'Okay, I can breath. I can live.'"

The next months and years were not easy. Roger began to show physical improvements but did not regain brain function in a way that made living at home safe for him or his family. The disappointing realities of traumatic brain injuries continued to chisel away at the hope of recovery. We all agreed to take special training with the doctors and nurses so we could assist in bringing Roger home for his first visit. Stefani continued to be optimistic that perhaps familiar surroundings could spark some recollection of his former life.

The day Roger came home was a hopeful day. Physically helping Roger get out of the car and attempt the steps into his home became the first of many obstacles. Then there was the complete lack of recognition of the family dog, the many beautiful pictures of his family, his creatively constructed backyard, or even his workshop. Most importantly, he had no recollection of Stefani or the kids. It was as if he would meet us all for the first time every time. It was crushing.

Stefani continued to hope, but her disillusionment grew as the reality of the situation became clearer. Caring for him was going to be impossible for the nonprofessionals: his adoring family. As the date approached when he would be discharged from the hospital, Stefani was advised to find a full-time care facility that specialized in the high-end care Roger needed. This is where he lives now.

In a drawn-out survival scenario, you will have to take responsibility over and over again as the situation changes around you. Shifting circumstances will also require you to keep reconfiguring your plan, as Stefani did. At first she was just blindly trying to get through the day. Eventually, she had to start thinking longer term about what she could control and what she had to let go.

Stefani's tenacity served her well. She describes herself as someone who always thought she could do it all. As the situation wore on, however, her tenacity had to be tempered by the realities of Roger's medical condition. Instead of running in all directions, Stefani had to check her desire to "fix" everything and evaluate where her time was best used. It became clear to her that, going forward, her kids had to be her focus.

Evaluate Your Survival Profile

Scientists have spent significant resources studying whether or not factors such as gender, race, age, socioeconomic status, and so forth affect your chances of survival in disasters. The answer is nuanced. Yes, there are some "profiles" that increase people's chances of survival, but only in certain situations. Even then, there is no magic profile of what a survivor looks like.

Amanda Ripley does an excellent job recapping "survivor profiles" in her book *The Unthinkable: Who Survives When Disaster Strikes—And Why*. Gender, weight, age, and income do statistically influence our chances for survival. One study she cites in chapter 4 of the book, for instance, found that 30 percent of men viewed the world from a low-risk perspective, making them much less cautious in survival situations.[8] In some scenarios this was helpful, as it inspired them to aggressive action. In other scenarios—for example, hurricanes—it is better to be among the cautious people who evacuate when prompted and get themselves to safety.

I can certainly relate to that 30-percent figure; my tendency is to be optimistic and perceive that the levels of risk for any situation are low, whether it is in my flights, my business, or my marriage. I know this about myself and try to train myself to think differently. I know that flying on a commercial airliner has the lowest statistical risk in travel, but I still tighten my seatbelt, read the emergency instructions, and pay attention to where the emergency exits are located. Why not? In the very small chance that something happens, I want to be prepared.

Controlling for gender, age, race, and other traits, people still perform differently in their levels of resilience. Through interviews and research, Ripley identified three "advantages" that determine someone's ability to be resilient. They are: "a belief that they can influence life events, a tendency to find meaningful purpose in one's turmoil, and a conviction that they can learn from both positive and negative experiences."[9]

What does this mean for you? Well, you do not need to fit yourself into a "survivor box", defining yourself as, for instance, "a medium-income white male, therefore . . ." You can spend some time, however, reflecting about your basic beliefs and attitudes. Regardless of gender or race, ask yourself questions like

---

8   Ripley cited Paul Slovic's *The Perception of Risk* (London: Earthscan Publications, 2000).

9   Ripley, *The Unthinkable*, 90–91.

these: Do you believe that you are in control of your fate? Do you believe that there is a bigger picture in suffering? And do you treat all experiences, good or bad, as opportunities for learning or building character?

Unearthing your basic tendencies is part of laying the groundwork of preparation for when your survival moment comes. As you evaluate your situation and make your plan, you will be able to remind yourself of some of your tendencies and either draw on them or correct for them in the situation. If you know that you have a high tolerance for risk, remind yourself of that before you go running into a house fire. Is this a smart survival choice or the result of your impulses?

I believe your predispositions carry weight in everyday survival situations as well. Are you someone who is overly cautious? Perhaps you are delaying making a decision that requires more urgency because you are uncomfortable with the amount of time you have in which to make the correct decision.

Ripley also makes the point that the way we *predict* we will act in survival situations is not often the way we end up acting. What is certain, however, is that we do carry all of our best and worst traits with us into our survival journey.

The Benefit of Practice

In the preceding discussion about discovering what your survivor profile looks like, I mentioned that, fortunately, we're able to correct some of the factors that hinder us or we're weakest in. One of the ways to do so is through training—and practice.

Let me give you a firsthand example of what I'm talking about. This mirrors what happened in the deadly case of the pilots of Air France Flight 447 (recall that incident from earlier in the chapter). When I experienced the same phenomenon in my own survival scenario, however, I fell back on my training.

I was landing heavily about 75 feet above the ground when my helicopter was struck by a rogue quartering tailwind. This caused the tail rotor on the helicopter, which keeps the fuselage from spinning in the opposite direction from the 300-mph blades, to quit being able to do its job. It was a hot day, and we were flying at a heavier than normal gross weight. The three factors were a deadly combination. We went into an uncontrolled spin.

Common sense would be to pull up on the controls, asking for more power to get out of the spin and fall. But the consequences of what seemed commonsensical would be deadly. Pulling up would aggravate the spin and further upset the helicopter's balance, making the helicopter spin so fast your vision would blur.

Instead of panicking, I let my training take over. I had practiced this very scenario many, many times in simulations: I put the helicopter into a collective down, taking the bite out of the blades and gaining some speed. This got us out of the downwash so that I could finally pull up a little. Even if I couldn't prevent an emergency landing, at least I would be able to lessen the impact and subsequent damage.

Endless repetition in aviation training was partially responsible for my ability to keep a clear head that day. In addition, before becoming a pilot I had done martial arts training. Thousands of years of martial arts wisdom emphasize practice: repetition and visualization. Over and over we did the same movements and visualized the scenarios in which we would use them. If an attacker jumped on us in an alleyway, our unconscious mind would ideally take over. We would execute the moves we had been taught, not giving our conscious minds any time to freeze or panic.

The training was incredibly repetitious and exhausting. I used to joke with my instructor that I was sure the endless training would save my life if only because, should someone try to jump me, I would be in prime shape to turn around and run the hell away.

Training to be a pilot works the same way. You get in front of the simulator and practice over and over ad nauseum. You make checklists and run through them again and again and again. You find out just how many times you can train with an engine out. I realize that not everyone wants to be a pilot, but this kind of preparation is useful in many kinds of survival situations, even the everyday.

For example, most of us frequently operate some type of motor vehicle. This is a much riskier operation than flying an airplane—or flying in one. (The National Safety Council's 2008 study put the odds of dying in a car accident at 1 in 98 over a lifetime versus 1 in 1,178 for flight.[10]) Every time you get into a car, you jeopardize your safety. Driving is probably the most risky activity you will do every day, but none of us think of it that way. If someone abruptly pulls out in front of you at an intersection or crosses the centerline, being able to execute defensive driving techniques could save your life.

Certain analytical minds love this kind of repetition; others find it very difficult. It's a bit like practicing for a standardized test. Many people don't enjoy taking practice tests, but

10 Aurelio Locsin, "Is Air Travel Safer than Car Travel?" *USA Today*. http://traveltips.usatoday.com/air-travel-safer-car-travel-1581.html.

the more times you practice SAT tests, the easier the real SAT will be on test day. You want to be so prepared that when the timer starts your conscious mind shuts off, and you go into execution mode, processing questions one solution at a time without panicking.

It's okay if you are one of those people who can't stand doing something twice. This is something to note about yourself when you find yourself shirking preparation. For myself, focusing on the positive reward and result of action versus the pain of inaction energizes me. If I start beating myself up about being lazy (inaction), I quickly lose steam. Sometimes it helps me to spend time visualizing the positive outcomes. Here's how prepared I "will" be once I put in the right amount of practice.

To be clear, you can't predict or practice for everything that life will throw at you. I can testify to that firsthand. Training and preparing yourself isn't about constantly imagining the worst-case scenario; it's about preparing for as many fire drills as you can. It's about knowing where your emergency exits are. It's about using tools like REACH so often that they become second nature. The message here is to seek to be prepared for a wide and unknowable set of circumstances, not to foster paranoia.

THE IMPORTANCE OF
YOUR WORK ETHIC

Too often in our culture we are sent messages that you can and should "have it all." It's as if each of us is owed success and all that comes with it—prestige, money, respect. We *all* have some sense of entitlement inherent in our own birthright. Welcome to the trap.

What gets you out of the trap of entitlement and into action is one very simple thing: plain, hard, and sometimes awful *work*. If you're not ready to work, you've lost before you've started. As Thomas Edison said, "Opportunity is sometimes missed because it is dressed in overalls and looks like work."

You can't delegate your success. *No one* with any character and self-respect, regardless of their socioeconomic standing, escapes this reality if they wish to achieve success on their own merits.

One gift I received early on was the opportunity to observe my parents' unstoppable work ethic. My mom was an emergency room head nurse in our small town. And my father, who had begun his career as an English teacher before becoming a serial entrepreneur and corporate executive, traveled often for work. Over the years, this often left my mom to handle on her own her full-time, high-intensity night shifts at the ER, a farm with nearly sixty boarded horses, a dozen other needy animals, two boys of her own plus four foster boys, and an intrepid though slightly built daughter who actively trained thousand-pound broncos.

As you can imagine, we were not the traditional meat and potatoes family. Nevertheless, the vegetable soup or very large tub of chili (which was meant to last all week) was always on the stove ready for us to eat. Somehow she kept it all together. My mom never complained and always faithfully filled in all the gaps. And when my dad would start yet another business and need an infusion of cash, it was my mom's hard-earned savings that would be coughed up.

Look around you. You will see those, like my parents, who get the job done no matter what. To their left and right are those who expect something for nothing. Unfortunately, most of us wear both hats. We choose between work and defeat over and over again, every day. We don't always choose right.

The next time you feel yourself procrastinating or recoiling from an opportunity because it will take time away from browsing the Internet or plopping yourself in front of the TV, which will you choose? Get your work ethic in shape now, because the stakes of *not* keeping up will be much higher when it's your survival that's in question.

Build Your Survival Cabinet

The leader of the free world has a cabinet of experts that he or she turns to for critical advice. You should too.

As you begin to evaluate your plan, you will start to tap inspirational and objective resources around you for wisdom and advice. Sometimes these resources will be authority figures in your life, like mentors, parents, or friends. Other times they will be more remote, like role models and survivors you have never yet you would strive to emulate.

Unless you are in very tough circumstances, your survival journey is not a solo one. Building a survival taskforce—a "Survival Cabinet," if you will—of the people best qualified to help you is a key element in your journey. You probably already have some kind of cabinet; just think who you go to when you have a problem you need help solving.

This isn't a setup, and you aren't obligated to follow all the advice your team gives you. In fact, some may even go unutilized, but you want a multitude of perspectives so the most objective strategy can be chosen among the plethora of possibilities.

It is unfortunate that people in tough situations are often reluctant to ask for help. They are either worried about imposing on others or inviting judgment upon their head for the mess in which they have found themselves. They might even be worried that other people don't want to help them. I understand where these fears come from, but you must overcome them if you want to succeed in your survival journey.

I want to stress that most people are honored to be asked for help. Why shouldn't they be, because in asking for help, you are acknowledging that you respect them. You are embracing humility and giving value to someone else's input. You have set aside your pride and are open to listening.

Fear of judgment should not hold you back. If there is one lesson you take from this book, it should be that everyone has a survival journey they must go on. Everyone hits a low point where they need help to get to the next step. Swallowing your maverick pride is the mark of a true survivor, not someone who lacks direction.

How you build and use your Survival Cabinet will have a

significant impact on your survival. The role of your cabinet is not to make survival decisions for you. You are still in charge of your own fate. Your advisers are there to act as a source of wisdom and a sounding board for your thinking. This is why you want the opinions of a wide range of people who know you in different capacities.

The benefit of asking people who know you well is that they can identify your blind spots and help you compensate for them. They know your style and can point out when you are adding to the problem. Be sure to also ask people you don't know as well for advice because doing so can yield more objective feedback. This is why you will want to look broadly for people you can trust for advice.

There is another strategic element in casting a wide net. Remember that everyone comes at a situation with his or her own biases and agendas. (See the box titled "Tunnel Vision" that follows for more on the effects of such preexisting biases and agendas.) Asking several people for feedback rather than just one person corrects for individual prejudices. And some consistent themes will emerge in the advice you are given as people tell you their stories. It's a numbers game; the more advice you get, the more refined your solution becomes. Pick and choose the survival elements from each conversation that will work for you

As the person in charge of your survival, it will be your job to weed the good advice from the bad. This is an important task, of course, as trusting the wrong person can be fatal. Sometimes your best resource is you. If you are being given advice that does not seem right, make different plans, even if it means disregarding someone whose opinion you respect. The responsibility is ultimately yours.

THE DANGERS OF TUNNEL VISION

Sometimes tunnel vision is not about a basic survival instinct but a previously existing goal we have that trumps everything else, even survival. In aviation we call this "get home-itis." I can't tell you how many times I've stood in front of a computer at a distant airport nervously studying a line of thunderstorms I just *had* to pierce in order to get home instead of doing the smart thing: delaying my return and waiting out the weather. This tendency kills many private pilots, especially pilots who commute via their private plane for business.

Mountaineering also has a specific term, "summit fever," to describe this exact phenomenon. A climber intent on bagging a peak will focus on summiting the mountain to the exclusion of such important factors as changing weather, broken gear, time elapsed, or their physical condition. Mountaineering disasters are often the result of someone pushing for the top even though evolving factors indicate that the level of risk has exponentially increased.

Such a catastrophe occurred on August 1 and 2, 2008, on K2, the second-highest mountain in the world. (The story is superbly told in *K2: Life and Death on the World's Most Dangerous Mountain* by Ed Viesturs and David Roberts.) Several expeditions of climbers were attempting their final day of climbing from the last camp to the summit. The day did not start well. Misplaced ropes created such significant delays that one expedition decided not to climb that day—a wise choice in retrospect. The rest pushed on.

In one of the most technical sections of the climb, the Bottleneck, an unclipped climber took a fall that proved fatal. Readjusting ropes and launching a recovery mission for the dead climber further delayed the climb. Still, most of the climbers kept marching toward the top of the mountain. Many of them achieved their goal. Eighteen climbers reached the summit, most of them around 8:00 P.M., *five hours* after the recommended summit time. After celebrating their success, the group turned around to descend the mountain in full darkness.

Negotiating the treacherous Bottleneck on the way down quickly became a nightmare. Though not all the circumstances are clear, falling ice and the difficulty of climbing this section at night certainly contributed to the disaster. Fixed ropes that the climbers were relying on in the descent were cut by the ice slides, leaving climbers stranded. Some opted to stay put. Others chose to free climb through the night without ropes. Neither option guaranteed survival.

The ice continued to fall from the mountain, wiping out entire expeditions that had tried to wait out the night. Those who decided to press on were unable to safely free climb the Bottleneck and fell to their deaths. A total of eleven climbers died and three others were seriously injured.

I don't relay the above story to illustrate how foolish the victims of the 2008 K2 climbing disaster were. These were experienced climbers, some of the best in the world. They had done the physical and mental preparation this kind of climb would require from them. Still, all their experience and skill was not enough to make them immune to mountaineering tunnel vision.

Several factors contributed. K2 is highly technical (much more so than Everest) and requires exceptional weather, making windows for summiting rare. Years go by where no summits are made.

Reaching the top of K2 is a special achievement in the climbing community. Because climbers spend all that money and effort to get to the mountain, they must feel immense pressure to achieve the dream. Very real red flags, like critical time delays, were not rationally processed because their brains were operating with one obsessive goal in mind: reach the top. The climbers' judgment was also probably impaired by fatigue and hypoxia (breathing with less oxygen). They were in a less-than-optimal state to make critical life-or-death decisions.

The story of the K2 climbers illustrates that throughout our lives we are asked to make decisions in difficult circumstances when we don't have all our faculties. Whether you are stressed, in mourning, or even on medication, you might have to come up with your survival plan in less than optimal headspace. The best you can do is to be aware of your limitations and be skeptical of your knee-jerk reactions.

When I decided to be pilot-in-command of the helicopter on the final day my ex-wife could appeal the divorce, I was not in the right frame of my mind to be taking on that kind of responsibility. My mind was fixated on the deadline, when flying needed my full attention. In the tradition of most aviation accidents, this wasn't the fatal mistake. Deciding to fly while distracted then adding on layers of other problems (the quartering tailwind, a warm day, etc.) was what got me in trouble. The K2 climbers lived a similar story. It is not one decision that gets you in trouble; it's the snowball effect when you've started out on shaky ground.

I believe we experience tunnel vision in everyday life as well. How many times have you insisted on driving home late at night when you are too tired to safely operate a vehicle? The goal becomes getting home, and changing circumstances, like your ability to stay awake, aren't properly factored in.

How often do you see people stay in unhealthy relationships because the goal becomes making the relationship work rather than the emotional health of either participant? I can attest to this firsthand: Midwestern values, pride, and a belief that I could barrel through any problem had me "tunneling" through a toxic marriage to the detriment of both parties and our children.

Survival can mean giving up on goals that we had previously established as the highest priority. A summit isn't worth your life. An unhealthy marriage isn't worth your happiness. Sometimes you have to accept that the mental chapter you wrote for yourself can no longer read like you expected or wanted it to.

Flying Solo

Should you be trapped in a situation where either an extreme timeline or isolation prevents you from asking others for help, you still have one key resource: your logical and creative self.

Fortunately, not being able to ask for advice in the moment doesn't mean you are stuck inventing a solution on your own. Remember, you can call on the experiences of past survivors to help guide you in your decision making.

At times, however, isolation will be even more extreme. You will not even have the example of past survivors to call upon. You are in uncharted territory. Your only resource is yourself. Flying solo doesn't mean you are at the end of your story. Slow things down. Don't let your emotions run wild. Don't freeze. Sequence things in the right manner—and get creative.

One of my favorite examples of survival in this kind of isolated scenario occurred in a remote area of Montana's Helena National Forest on August 5, 1949. (The story dramatically unfolds in Norman Maclean's excellent *Young Men and Fire*.)

Fifteen US Forest Service smokejumpers had been deployed to combat a wilderness fire about half a mile from Mann Gulch. Upon arrival, the smokejumpers created a plan for their afternoon of work, taking into account the terrain and the conditions.

As the men descended into the narrow gulch toward the Missouri River, the strong winds suddenly changed direction. Whereas before they had a clear exit strategy should something go wrong, they were now trapped against the steep walls of the canyon with the fire headed straight at them. Even worse, high temperatures and an abundance of dry grass in the direction whence the wind was now blowing created perfect conditions for a "blow-up," that is, a fast-moving wildfire. In the next ten minutes, the fire would cover 3,000 acres.

The foreman, Wagner Dodge, immediately reoriented his men away from the fire to begin moving up the canyon, ordering them to drop their tools. Interestingly, not all complied, refusing to give up their heavy equipment ("freezing") until it was forcibly taken from them. Dodge realized that even running at a full sprint without their tools they would not make it to the top of the ridge before getting incinerated, so he made a split-second decision.

Faced with an oncoming wall of flame, Dodge lit his own fire in the dry grass and then stepped into it, clearing a wide circle of brush around him. He shouted at his men to follow his example, but most thought he had just gone crazy. Certainly he had to maintain his confidence to follow *his* plan and not succumb to the majority's panicked scramble up the steep hillside.

Only three of the men survived. Two miraculously found crevices in the ridge walls in which to take shelter; the rest of the men were trapped in the fire below. The final survivor—overtaken by the raging fire but not burned alive—was Dodge.

What Dodge had done was nothing short of miraculous. By lighting his own fire, he had burned the brush around him away before the quick-moving wildfire was upon him. The wildfire burned around him but not over him in his cleared patch.

His technique for creating a burned-out "safe space" in the fire was not part of Forest Service protocol. In later questioning, when asked why he'd done what he did, Dodge explained that, while he'd never heard of anyone using this technique, at the time, it just seemed "logical" to him. As Maclean writes in his moving book on the disaster, Dodge invented the solution on the spot.

Unfortunately Wagner Dodge is not alive to interview today. I would have liked to hear more about how he responded so quickly and innovatively to the disaster he was facing. He is a prime example of facing sure death, reacting as calmly as possible, and coming up with an entirely new survival technique—of being your own source of wisdom.

President of the Survival Cabinet

Building your Survival Cabinet can become a full-time job if you find yourself out of your depth. One of my good friends, LT Slater, did just that. Since 2009 he has had a troubling history of chronic illness. It began when he experienced an excruciating pain in his back—like "someone had shoved a knife in." It went away, but then those sharp jabs started to happen frequently and at longer intervals. His family practice doctor was unable to diagnose the problem, and the first specialist he consulted couldn't help either. Neither could the next. In the end he was simply prescribed pain medication and sent on his way.

The Slater Family, LT Slater's motivation.

Around the same time, LT's father was diagnosed with Stage 4 non-Hodgkin's lymphoma. This set off alarm bells for

LT. Feeling uneasy, he asked his doctor whether he could also have cancer given the family connection, but his doctor wrote off his concern. LT decided to take a more proactive stance on his health. After all, he and his wife had a young child with another on the way; he was also the president of two growing companies.

So LT applied for more insurance and then, via YPO, tapped into a specialized network of spine doctors who could hopefully help him untangle his chronic pain.

These doctors did a deeper dive—and unearthed troubling results: LT had a significant mass in his chest, Stage 4 Hodgkin's lymphoma. LT was immediately put on a treatment plan. LT had been present for many of his father's treatments, so the "unknown" factor was much less scary. The good news was that LT's cancer was very treatable.

The first order of business was for LT and his wife to have their second child. "We timed it so I did my first chemotherapy and then had a C-section a week later. That was a bit of a unique scenario," he says. The upside of a grueling six-month chemo regimen was that he spent most of his time at home with his wife and newborn baby. His older daughter was supposed to start kindergarten but stayed home as well so as not to bring home classroom sicknesses. "We were really lucky to have that time together."

The initial treatment was successful, but not for long. The cancer came back. LT went back for another round of chemotherapy and then a bone marrow transplant. He went another year in remission when the cancer came back a third time. The doctors diagnosed that his immune system was failing him. The only way to survive was to have his immune system replaced altogether, meaning that he needed another bone marrow transplant preceded by more chemotherapy.

LT was given a new drug that seemed to do the trick and found a perfect ("twelve point") match in his brother as a bone marrow donor. But, the guarantees of surviving the transplant or the new immune system—which had the potential to attack his body—were low. "You can stay in the building and burn to death, or jump off the building and hope to survive. That's sort of your options. I knew for a fact I couldn't survive based on the available treatments," LT explained. The gamble was a tough one, but LT knew he didn't really have a choice. "Your life is about more than just you," LT says. "The obvious target is the kids. There wasn't a choice whether to fight this or not."

The good news is that today LT is technically cancer-free. He is humbly optimistic. "I'm in the light at the end of the tunnel, I just have a few webs to shake off."

When speaking to LT, what strikes you, other than his overwhelming positivity, is his encyclopedic knowledge of his medical conditions and the associated treatments: the drugs he is on or the technical aspects of the medical procedures he's undergone.

"You need to be your own strongest advocate. Ask your questions and do your research. Even if you think you have the best doctor in the world, question what your doctor is telling you. You have to have great advisers. That means family. That means friends. That means psychological expertise. You don't have to be going through life-threatening issues to have sounding boards like that."

This is a man who very carefully built his cabinet and then became an expert in his own right. LT is a perfect example of having control in an uncontrollable situation.

Reacting to survival situations in a calm, collected manner is no easy task. Some of us have a leg up. Perhaps we are in a profession that trains us to handle crises. Or, we are fortunate enough genetically to be disposed to weather trauma well.

Even if you do not have these advantages, you are not doomed to be a victim of disasters. You can actively work to improve your survival stats by spending time reflecting on how you respond to stress and conflict. Knowing your own Survivor Profile, getting fitness and readiness training, and learning and applying the REACH protocol are great ways to get started.

It is also smart to have potential nominees lined up for your Survival Cabinet before you even need them. Who are people you would approach if something went seriously wrong in your life? What resources and relationships, mentors or otherwise, could you do a better job of cultivating? How would you go about asking for help?

For me, it was difficult to admit that I had failed as a pilot, husband, father, and business partner. But, by divulging that information to members of my Survival Cabinet, I reaped the benefit of key stakeholders who were truly invested in my life and progress. Even past my survival experience, they continue to enrich my life with their wisdom.

Put all your preventative measures in place before disaster strikes. This isn't being paranoid, it's being smart. But understand that, depending on the circumstances, there's only so much preparation you can do. This book will not make or break your survival; you will. You will have to use every resource you can to create the best survival plan while keeping yourself calm and rational.

CHAPTER 3

ACTION

Chris was now trapped in the breezeway between a wounded student and a psychopath.

The shooter didn't give Chris any time to speak before putting a bullet in him. The force of the bullet drove Chris back. Then he was shot again, this time in the finger.

"That's what you get for calling the cops!"

What to do next? Chris tried pleading with the guy, explaining that he hadn't called the cops. Someone else had notified them as soon as the first shots were fired. They were already on their way. It was time for the rampage to stop.

In response, the shooter aimed his gun at the phone Chris gripped in his hand.

He decided to make one last appeal.

"It's my kid's birthday, man!"

Evaluation in the REACH protocol requires slowing down and making a step-by-step plan for your survival. The next element, *action*, however, requires a 180-degree turn. You have made your well-considered plan; now it is Go Time.

Once you are in the right state of mind and have committed to a plan, you should waste no time carrying it out. A few seconds of hesitation can mean the difference between survival and defeat. This is particularly true in extreme survival situations when you are faced with the literal oncoming train. But, this truth is relevant for everyday survival as well. Dragging your feet before facing your issues is normal, but problems only get worse as you let them fester. Our natural tendency is to hesitate before jumping in; your job is to overcome that.

In this chapter we will also discuss what *action* means— the concept is probably more nuanced than you think. Action doesn't always translate into something aggressive or physical. Your plan might be as simple as considering the options, then waiting for the right circumstances before choosing what you deem the best option. "Acting" can mean settling yourself down for the long haul until it is time to move to the next stage of the plan.

No matter whether your actions are thoughts or deeds, remember these prophetic words of Benjamin Disraeli: "Action may not always bring happiness, but there is no happiness without action."

The stories in this chapter will highlight the necessity of immediately kicking your plan into motion. You will read about the survivors of a shark attack, the first commercial hijacking, and a mine collapse in Chile. These survivors created a plan and chose to continue to execute it every step of the way. They did not waste time. They did not second-guess themselves. They acted. Their urgency and commitment made the difference in their survival.

No Time To Think

Once you have your plan, immediate action is required. For most people, this is not easy. You will start questioning what you have decided to do. Do I have all the information? Am I making the right choice? What happens if my plan goes awry? This is natural, but it is not helpful. You cannot hesitate if you want to survive. My friend Mario, one of the key members of my Survival Cabinet, explains this well: We can't stop time, so if you know something is coming, do something about it *now*. Survivors decide on their plan and then make it happen.

Action ties strongly to the first letter in the acronym REACH, *responsibility*. It is your *responsibility* not just to *act*, but to *act now*. My friend John DiJulius, in his excellent book *The Customer Service Revolution*, explains *why* we are all obligated to aggressively and passionately pursue survival. John dislikes the phrase, "I tried my best." To him: "'Doing your best' is a mistaken measurement for achievement. Your 'best' has a ceiling on it set by whatever you've been able to achieve in the past. Instead, we all have an obligation to live beyond our best. We owe it to ourselves and to the people we can help by embracing a full, productive, and service-oriented life."

John takes this responsibility so seriously that he has written a personal purpose statement for himself that he has taped up all over his house: "Live an extraordinary life so countless others do as well."

When you wonder why you have to *act*, why you can't delay, think about John's purpose statement—and what your own might be. When it comes to survival, you aren't just risking your own life, but everything you have to offer. When it comes to survival, your best is not enough. You can live extraordinarily beyond your best if *you* choose to do so. Look at each and every one of the survivors I've included in this book. They all lived beyond what they thought, originally, was their "best."

Do or Die

In long-term survival scenarios, the importance of swift execution is hard to see if the risk to your life is not imminent. In immediate, short-term survival scenarios, needing to act is black-and-white. You move out of the way of the train or you die. You evacuate the burning building or you risk immolation. Your split-second reaction still counts as *evaluation*; you are choosing not to freeze or panic. But, whatever you do, you do it quickly, because that split-second reaction counts as *action* as well. One moment of hesitation could make the difference in your survival.

Halloween 2014. Brian Wargo and his friend McKenzie Clark were surfing in Keawaeli Bay in North Kohala, Hawaii, when McKenzie was attacked by a tiger shark. The 12-foot shark initially bit into her surfboard, grabbing her fingers in the process. Without letting go, the shark began to swim out to sea, dragging along the board and McKenzie with it. Brian watched, horrified, unable to aid his friend. Before she was taken too far out, the shark dropped the board and kept swimming.

Instead of swimming for shore and getting to safety, Brian swam to McKenzie, directing her to get back on her board before the shark returned. Brian knew that tiger sharks are aggressive, so he was prepared when he saw the shark turn around to make another pass at McKenzie. As the shark swam by him, Brian grabbed it by the dorsal fin. He began relentlessly punching it in the gills, figuring this was his best chance of stopping the attack.

Brian didn't let up, and after about the fifth punch the shark had finally had enough. It left, this time for good, he hoped. His next priority was getting the injured McKenzie to shore. With the aid of two more surfers, Brian helped her swim in and quickly made a tourniquet for her bitten hand. McKenzie was later treated at a hospital, losing part of one finger due to the bite and receiving stitches. She considers herself lucky to be alive.

Even if the chances of any of us being attacked by a shark are low, I believe the value in studying these stories is that they starkly underscore the necessity of action: do or die. When asked about the shark attack in an interview with *Reader's Digest*, Brian explained, "I knew what I had to do to save my friend."[11] For him it was this simple. Whatever the risk to himself, he leapt to action without a second thought. Both he and McKenzie owe their survival to his determination.

We learn from these survivors that swift action should be a key piece of the mentality each of us should try to cultivate, even in everyday survival situations. If your problem took the form of an attacking shark, what would you do? Do you freeze, panic, or do you actively defend yourself and your loved ones before the situation worsens? Use the metaphor of taking the shark by the dorsal fin to inspire you. Every problem is a shark swimming by. In everyday survival scenarios—especially ones that are drawn out over time—it will be critical to keep operating with this decisive mindset.

---

11 Katie Askew, "This Surfer Punched a Shark to Save His Friend," *Reader's Digest*, September 2015.

Committed to the Long Haul

In a long-term survival situation, decisive action looks a little different than the split-second survival scenario. Your choice to carry out your plan isn't a singular one. There will be many forks in the road where you will decide whether to keep on or call it quits.

I first heard Frank Iszak's story while listening to NPR. I was so fascinated I had to pull my car over to the side of the road to give the interview the attention it deserved. Because of his desire to help others, Iszak was incredibly generous in agreeing to be interviewed for this book.

Frank Iszak

Born in Hungary he became an adult during the Communist regime there. A repression of civil liberties and the use of secret police and work camps to punish non-compliant citizens meant that Hungarians lived each day in fear. Iszak grew up wanting to be a writer. Instead, he was sent to university to study chemical engineering. There he found an outlet for his passion for writing by contributing to the school newspaper, penning articles critical of the school and the oppressive regime. These were not well received.

When he was forced to quit the school paper, Iszak continued writing at an independent newspaper, openly espousing anti-Communist views. This got him sent to a uranium mine ("slave labor," as he describes it). He escaped half a year into his "sentence" and began working as a laborer at a brick factory under faked paperwork.

Just twenty-five years old, his prospects were extremely limited. As Iszak explains it, "I had nowhere to go. I was at the crosshairs of the regime." The one bright spot in his life was his marriage to twenty-three-year-old Anais, who shared his dream of a life free of oppression and terror.

Rather than continuing to wait for the other shoe to drop, Iszak decided it was time to cross the Iron Curtain and find a better life for them both beyond. He would *make* it happen. (That was certainly a demonstration of taking *responsibility*.) He figured his best bet was to commandeer a plane and fly to freedom. When he ran his radical idea by Anais, her only question was when could they leave.

What followed were eight months of assiduous planning (*evaluation*). Iszak had carefully shared his plans to defect with his friend George Polyak, a former fighter pilot. George also wanted in and became responsible for the technical elements of the plan, as Iszak knew nothing about flying. In fact, he had never even been on a plane. "I was working on the spirit of the plan. I was the motivator," he explained. They recruited several more compatriots.

As it turned out, their plan was more like the framework of a plan. They could only guess at the number of passengers who would be on the plane, including the pilots and a secret policeman. They could also only hazard a guess as to what the pilots might do once they realized the plane was being hijacked. Missing were critical details such as what the cockpit door would be made of (if it were steel they would not be able to force their way through); if there would be seatbelts; where, exactly, the secret policeman—who they would have to overcome—would be sitting. They didn't even really know where they would land. Their hope was that they would end up outside the Iron Curtain, not the side of a mountain.

Although the unknowns were significant, Iszak was not deterred. He had evaluated his situation within Hungary and decided that the risk of this hijacking was still less than the risk of continuing to live under the Communist regime. He and Anais and his five friends committed as a group to see their survival plan through.

Their commitment would be tested time and again. As Iszak shared with me, "It's easy to commit—unless you *really* commit." In other words, it's easy to talk a big talk; it is much harder to follow through.

Iszak viewed the group's risks on three levels: their own safety (he was sure they would be tortured and executed should the plan fail or should they be betrayed; additionally, there was no guarantee that George could fly or land the plane); the safety of the innocent passengers on the plane who would unwittingly be involved in the hijacking; and the safety of their friends and family left back home, who might be punished for the defectors' actions.

Iszak's determination to carry out the hijacking was tested

right up until takeoff. On July 13, 1956, the seven defectors boarded a commercial flight with a total of nineteen people on board. The plane started down the runway and Iszak felt himself panicking. "For a moment, I was going to yell 'Stop!' before we had even started," he said. "But my mind overruled that." Even worse, however, was when their takeoff was momentarily aborted because a white police van pulled alongside the plane. Iszak was sure they had been betrayed. It turned out to simply be some last-minute cargo to place in the hold. The hijacking would continue.

The plane took off and the hijackers immediately went into action. They knocked out each and every one of the other passengers: better safe than sorry, since they were not sure which one was the secret policeman. They then rushed the cockpit. Luck was on their side; theirs was an older plane whose cockpit door was made of wood rather than steel.

Unfortunately, the secret policeman had been sitting up with the pilots rather than with the passengers, which the hijackers had not counted on. He aimed his pistol at them and pulled the trigger. The gun misfired, narrowly missing them and leaving two holes in the ceiling. George rushed him and was able to wrestle him down.

The pilots then executed emergency procedures, plunging the plane toward the ground. "The plane came down from 4,000 to 800 feet," Iszak recalled. The result was chaos, people flying through the cabin. "There was an incredible cracking, falling, floating. You have no control. The plan is out the window. Then you panic; but it is just a moment. *There is no action from panic.*"

George wrenched the controls from the pilots and brought the plane back to 10,000 feet. With the plane under their control but quickly losing fuel, the group flew over the Alps into thunderstorms, hoping to escape any pursuers but also not to crash straight into a mountain as they bounced around in the extreme turbulence. Just as they were about to run out of fuel, the clouds cleared and a runway appeared. It was a miracle. George landed the plane. Everyone was alive, although significantly worse for the wear (Anais, for example, had suffered a broken leg).

There remained one last piece of the plan to execute. The group was not sure *where* they had actually landed the plane. For all they knew, they could still be within the Communist Bloc. Out of the mist a vehicle began rumbling toward them with a gun fixed to the top. If they hadn't made it beyond the Iron Curtain, they were facing a painful, slow death; they would be made examples of what happens when you try to defect.

Iszak still had the old pistol. He cocked the trigger and held it to his wife's head, prepared to take her life and his own rather than be imprisoned, as they had discussed. "That was the heaviest moment ever in my life," he said, "to put the gun to her head and have my index finger a millimeter or two away from killing her and myself."

Their luck still held. As the Jeep came closer they saw it was painted with the stars and stripes. They had landed on a new NATO Air Force base in West Germany. They were free.

Iszak's survival journey is a blockbuster, beyond what most of us can imagine. What impressed me most from hearing his experiences was his commitment to *action* every step of the way. Even when he panicked, he refocused and let his rational mind take control. The moment passed and he was rewarded with his freedom.

You may not agree with the ethics or tactics of any given survivor (i.e. Nando Parrado and cannibalism or Frank Iszak and hijacking). But, their decisions reinforce the reality that your survival is not always black and white. Difficult decisions in gray moral zones must be made and acted on.

Take Action . . . Sit Tight

The other significant difference between short-term and long-term survival scenarios is that "taking action" doesn't always look swift and aggressive, like punching a shark or overwhelming a plane full of people. Even in Frank Iszak's story, there were moments when taking action and executing his plan simply meant choosing not to give in to panic or give up altogether.

The extreme end of counterintuitive action is where "acting" translates to "strategically waiting." Sometimes you aren't hesitating or being paralyzed by fear, you simply need to wait for circumstances to change before you can make your next move. At other times you are truly out of options. All you can do is make a prolonged plan for hunkering down and hope for rescue—as the following white-knuckle story clearly illustrates.

On August 5, 2010, at the San José mine in Chile's Atacama desert, a block of diorite rock forty-five stories tall loosened and smashed through critical layers of the mine, crushing the tunnel ramp that served as the mine's exit. One man near the mine entrance managed to escape the falling rock by driving out of the mine at full speed, but the rest of the crew was not so lucky. Thirty-three miners had become trapped 2,300 feet below the surface.

Mercifully, the rock did not fall all at once, which allowed all the men to get to safety in the Refuge, a reinforced chamber near the bottom of the mine. Nevertheless, they knew they were in trouble. Reactions among the men varied: One group went to scout out the damage and to evaluate the situation, particularly whether or not they could access the escape shafts. Others panicked, however, descending on the meager emergency food stores kept in the Refuge. Within several minutes, they wiped out several days' worth of provisions.

Eventually the scouting group rejoined the men in the Refuge. The news was bad: The diorite slab had effectively cut off multiple levels of the spiraling ramp that enabled transit through the mine. The emergency shafts built into the mine were similarly cut off. There was no way out of the mine. They were stuck in the dark waiting for rescue without knowing if or when that would ever come.

The news was devastating to the men. A few immediately assumed they were sealed in a living tomb where they would starve, suffocate, or be crushed by another rockfall. Several men argued that they should explore the emergency shafts. But the mine was not done shifting. Further exploration was too dangerous to the climbers and the rest of the men, in the event their efforts to escape destabilized the mine further.

The calmer men in the group began to take charge. One of the more charismatic among them, a miner named Sepulveda, addressed the group. "We're in deep shit. The only thing we can do is be strong, superdisciplined, and united."[12] The men agreed. They began to make plans, recognizing that while they waited to be rescued, they needed to keep themselves alive and as healthy as possible.

First the men took inventory of the food, creating a rationing plan that would last them about a week. (A week turned out to

---

12 Hector Tobar, "Sixty-Nine Days," *The New Yorker*, July 7, 2014.

be an incredibly optimistic estimate of the length of time the miners would spend trapped below the surface.)

When they were not consuming their meager rations or listening for signs of rescue, they had to find other ways to keep calm and committed to survival. The men employed various coping strategies, from prayer to sleep to jogging in the mine. Anything that would allow them to psychologically weather the torture of being sealed thousands of feet from the surface. They kept to their rationing plan religiously, some men even eating less then their allotted portion to make the food stretch a little longer.

On the third day of entrapment, they began to hear drills boring into the rock above them. This added another strategic element to their waiting: should a drill bit break through, they would need to let their rescuers far above them know they were alive. The miners found a can of red spray paint with which to paint the bit and prepared written notes with information about their condition and location that they could affix to the drill. If the drill broke through, they would be prepared.

After weeks of living nearly half a mile underground, after repeatedly listening to drills narrowly miss their small chamber, on the seventeenth day of the rescue efforts, a drill broke through. The men celebrated wildly and then got down to business, knowing exactly what to do based on their planning. They spray-painted the drill bit red and then planted their notes into different crevices on the drill, praying that the paint and paper would survive the long ride to the surface.

When the drill was retracted, rescuers found a note they never expected: "We are well in the Refuge. The 33." Another celebration erupted aboveground as well.

The miners' fight for survival was not over. Their extraction could not be immediate. The drill operators worked around the clock to excavate a tunnel large enough to safely transport the men from the Refuge to the surface in a specially designed capsule. The miners potentially were facing months down in the mine, but at least they were now supplied with food and other comforts. Fifty-seven days later, all thirty-three men were brought to the surface alive.

The survival journey of the Chilean miners is an amazing testament to human resilience, technological prowess, and cooperation in the face of disaster (the rescue effort was international). It is also an important example of what you can do when your survival depends on others. Ultimately, releasing the trapped miners came down to whether or not the rescue efforts were successful. But the rescue would have been for nothing if the miners themselves hadn't acted on their own behalf to stay alive and cooperate with their rescuers on the surface.

The miners could have panicked and eaten all the food stores outright or given into hunger after a week and depleted their food supply at that point. They could have continued to senselessly explore the blocked tunnels and been injured or killed by falling rock. Instead, they came up with a plan for rations and signaling to the rescuers. They put their faith in a rescue. And they waited.

Alternatively, if you're forced to play a waiting game, the action you take can be unrelated to your specific survival circumstance but still help you move forward. For example, in the midst of my divorce battle when my business was frozen due to financial restraining orders, I got up and went to "work" for my favorite charities. Selfishly, this was an excellent diversion from my own struggles. I had a purpose and a positive impact when I was otherwise helpless. Doing this work also helped me have a different perspective on my own struggles. The suffering I saw in my nonprofit work was far beyond what I was going through.

One Step at a Time: Reset Your Goals, Make Another Plan, and Sail Forward

One of the most important lessons I learned from my divorce battle was to reset my goals as factors that were outside my control changed the direction the situation was going.

I think this lesson is true for any survival journey. Any transition (a gentler word for survival) encompasses a never-ending cycle of changing perspectives and goals. To move on, we adapt by resetting our expectations. Survival on Day 1 can look a lot different from Survival on Day 40 (or, in my case, Day 800).

When my divorce was final, my life and estate were not just scorched embers and ashes, but something worse. I owed $50 million in debts and obligations. An unfathomable number. How was I ever, ever going to get out of this hole? It would have been easy to declare bankruptcy, an option some well-meaning friends and family members who had stood by me through all the carnage advised.

While I don't fault people who file for bankruptcy, this was a major point of stubbornness for me. For one, I believed that filing for bankruptcy was actually an inaccurate representation of our investment portfolio. Real estate had been hit hard, but I felt that the dip was temporary and our properties would regain their value. I wanted to ride out the storm rather than scuttle the ship. It was also a point of integrity for me. Declaring bankruptcy would have sent shockwaves through my partnership groups that trusted me with their money.

Looking at the work ahead of me, I told Gina that she should feel no obligation to stay by my side. She was talented and beautiful and had her whole life ahead of her. We had started dating in the midst of my long divorce battle, and she had already been through so much. Why waste it waiting for me or getting dragged through more mud?

She wasn't having it. She was confident that we would have a happy life together, no matter what that meant. I was ashamed. My former identity had been tied up so completely in my net worth that I was still shaking off my bruised ego.

My father reminded me that there were other people who were struggling with much worse things than I was. I needed to love my kids, love my new relationship with Gina, and get ready to jump back in the ring once the markets picked up. That was my duty.

Between Gina, my father, my sons, my Survival Cabinet, my YPO group, and all the rest of my loving family and friends, I felt like I'd been given permission to hit "Reset." I could take time to assess what the next step was in my new reality instead of frantically getting back in the ring. The whole extended family appreciated the new humble me as I became more invested in enriching relationships instead of imprisoning myself in my work.

With this new confidence, I decided *not* to file for bankruptcy. My new goal was to show up at the office and "fake it until I make it." Earlier in my career I had defined success as increasing my net worth by $50 million. Now, however, my new goal was to fight for a zero balance. I went to work every day and methodically and aggressively chipped away on the road to a strangely uplifting $0!

If the goal had been any more ambitious, I think I would

have found myself overwhelmed. The divorce had taken its toll on me. Trying to rebuild the wealth I had lost would have been the equivalent of launching myself straight at Mount Everest after taking a decade off from climbing. Working myself back to zero was like warming up on the foothills before tackling the real thing.

Incremental success fueled my confidence. (I'll share more about this in the very next chapter, titled "Confidence") I rebuilt my business, I came to work every day refreshed and feeling more and more like I was ready to up the ante.

The whole journey felt a little like sailing a boat. I had no control over the movement of the wind or waves; I had to tack and react to these changes in the environment in order to eventually make it to port—and not necessarily the port I'd set out for. Storms kicked up. I got blown off course. The journey would be irretrievably altered. But every alteration was a chance to reassess where I was going and how I would get there.

Breaks in the journey—the chance to rest and refuel before moving on again—were necessary and something to be valued. Those small breaks gave me a chance to come up with and implement new strategies, even if they were as simple as "fighting for zero."

Taking action is not a complicated concept. All that stops you are your own fears. Trust yourself. If you have done your best to create an informed, reasonable survival plan, you must now execute that plan. You must push past procrastination; dragging your feet is the easier thing to do, but it could have dire consequences for you and others in your survival journey.

My hope is that the stories in this chapter underscored how

important it is to act without hesitation. Deciding to leave your family behind and defect by hijacking an airplane is not easy. Can you imagine Iszak's angst at executing his plan when leaving his parents behind could endanger *their* lives due to punishments imposed by the government in retaliation? Or the idea that landing on the wrong side of the Iron Curtain would certainly cost him and Anais their lives? I know the pain I caused my family by dragging out the divorce process rather than putting an end to the toxic situation much earlier.

Confronting an aggressive shark is not easy. Neither is getting a divorce. But what you are risking by *not* acting is much greater. Ask yourself these questions: "What is the worst-case scenario if I do nothing? What am I risking if I do not act? Who will be affected?"

You can tie this line of questioning back to our first REACH element, *responsibility*. Just like Chris Mintz's final motivation to act were thoughts of his son, ask yourself: "Who else is going to lose out if I am not successful on my survival journey? Who is depending on me? Who needs me? Whose life will be forever impacted if I am gone? What could I still accomplish or contribute?" Your answers to these soul-searching questions are your *why*. Use that to find the courage to implement your survival plan.

CHAPTER 4

CONFIDENCE

Chris had been shot as though he were an extra in a video game. His legs were "like ice." When he tried to move, he described the pain as a bomb going off within him.

Five bullets. One in his abdomen. One in his finger. One in his shoulder blade. And one in each leg.

The gunfire had finally stopped. It became apparent that the perpetrator had been apprehended as people began coming out of their hiding places. Emergency responders soon took over. But Chris had ceased to have any sense of time. What felt like an eternity, however, was actually less than ten minutes.

One of Chris's friends noticed him and knelt down beside him. Chris asked her to call his son's mother and let her know he couldn't pick up his son from school that day.

An EMT walked by; Chris, in his fogginess, realized he knew the guy. It was a good friend of his.

"Hey buddy," Chris whispered.

"Hey," his friend responded.

A friendly face. Chris's ordeal—nightmare—was over. He was in caring and competent hands.

With that, Chris felt himself let go. "I KNEW WE WERE ALL GOING TO BE OKAY," he wrote later.

A key factor particularly in the action element of REACH is for you to have *confidence* that your survival plan will work. If you start acting out a plan but distrust yourself or doubt that plan you will infinitely increase the stress in your survival journey. That anxiety might further cloud your thinking and lead you to make poor choices or to procrastinate. Trust yourself, your ability to make decisions, and your ability to execute your plan. There will always be plenty of naysayers. Stay the course by practicing this little exercise: Inhale confidence. Exhale doubt.

Confidence can be a double-edged sword, though. Over-confidence or misplaced confidence has the potential to get you into trouble. Many times people find themselves in survival situations because they have overestimated their own abilities, underestimated the factors outside their control, or trusted historical outcomes without paying enough attention to their present circumstances. While a large part of this chapter will be devoted to the importance of having confidence, the ways it can burn you will also be discussed.

The stories in this chapter cover a wide range of survival scenarios: exploring the Amazon, becoming trapped in a submerged boat at the bottom of the sea (really), and suffering frostbite while summiting Mount Everest. In each story confidence plays a pivotal role; sometimes, misplaced confidence is the impetus for disaster. In all the cases, however, confidence in a survival plan is what gets everyone safely through.

When you are fighting for your life, it can be difficult to strongly believe in your own resourcefulness. This isn't uncommon; there are a lot of victims out there whose mindset is telling them they can't do it. The one surefire way to stop doubting and restore *confidence* in your ability to survive is to go back to the first step you took in REACH: *responsibility*. In other words, confidence is slowly built as you *evaluate* your options and commit to your own survival plan. Each time you decide to take *action* and then follow through, you gain more certainty in your own abilities. *Responsibility, evaluation,* and *action* are stepping-stones to building confidence in your abilities and yourself.

By the end of this chapter, you will better understand how critical confidence is in your survival journey—and how to use it properly.

Confidence: A Balancing Act

Having confidence in yourself is essential to surviving calamities great and small, but you don't ever want to make plans solely based on feelings of confidence. Remember, your careful, broad analysis and *evaluation* of circumstances were what enabled you to decide upon a plan. Confidence is what will enable you to see your plan through. Don't fall prey to complacency, dogma, or— as in my case, sometimes—just the lack of commitment.

Sometimes people over-rely on their confidence. They allow an unrealistic appraisal of their abilities to determine their actions. Or, their inflated view of themselves results in their underestimation of such uncontrollable factors as the weather. People also run the risk of deriving a false confidence from their past experiences. I see this in business all the time. Recall our snake in the woods analogy in chapter 1? If you've hiked that trail a hundred times and have never seen a snake, you don't expect to see one. Even worse, you become confident that you can hike that trail with no problems—and thus you don't prepare for any. You have created a false sense of security.

These three tendencies—overconfidence in our own abilities, underestimating the unknown, and trusting historical outcomes—mark the ways in which confidence can lead you astray. While you must be confident in your survival plan, you must also be vigilant that you don't fall into one of these traps.

Danger #1: Overconfidence in Our Own Abilities

Overconfidence is often responsible for people getting into survival situations in the first place. Recall from chapter 2 the mention of mountaineers who get "summit fever" and narrowly focus on making the top of the mountain at all costs? Part of the issue is that they have too much confidence in their climbing abilities. As factors like weather or darkness complicate their plans, they continue to believe in their ability to climb safely. Sometimes the most experienced mountaineers make the most rash choices. Having survived many climbs in the past, they think they will always win.

If you have a leader who is prone to overconfidence, entire groups of people can end up compromised. One of my favorite stories that illustrates this truth is Teddy Roosevelt's 1913–14 trip down the Amazon River as told in Candice Millard's *The River of Doubt: Theodore Roosevelt's Darkest Journey*. Roosevelt is a man we celebrate for his grandiosity and bravery—but sometimes I wonder why. Sure, his confidence provided him with a lifetime of adventures, but his recklessness and arrogance endangered lives. Was he brave, or was he a total buffoon?

Fresh from losing his third presidential campaign, Roosevelt was offered an opportunity by the Brazilian government to journey down the Amazon on a trip sponsored by the American Museum of Natural History. He accepted with enthusiasm, excited at the prospect of collecting natural specimens and touring the great river.

Roosevelt anticipated this trip to be a fun "return-to-boyhood" rather than a serious expedition. Consequently, he took little interest in planning it, delegating the logistics instead to a man named Anthony Fiala, who had a day job as a department store clerk. Fiala's explorer credentials were hardly inspiring: he had led but one expedition in the Arctic, and it was a failure of epic proportions. Leader and crew were trapped on the ice for *two years* before being rescued!

Upon his arrival in Brazil, Roosevelt was offered the chance to head down the unmapped, unexplored Rio da Duvida (River of Doubt). He eagerly accepted, throwing out the original plan for the expedition in favor of this new route. This was not the first time an expedition would attempt the River of Doubt; several had set off in previous years and been beset by disease, starvation, and encounters with hostile natives. Few survived.

Roosevelt set off with characteristic enthusiasm, deaf to his sponsors' and family's concerns. Bad weather plagued the expedition from the outset, and with the torrential rains came ill health (malaria, in particular) and mud, making it almost impossible to transit the trails. The expedition began to abandon equipment and frivolous culinary supplies along with most of their canoes. It was not long before everyone was on half-rations. Still they pressed on.

Only a quarter of the way through their journey and walking barely six miles a day, the men were already on the brink.

Frequently portaging the river's unexpected rapids had immeasurably slowed their journey. Insects, lack of food, surveillance by natives, and disease were taking their toll. The journey home became a race against time.

Circumstances became desperate when Roosevelt injured himself—gashing his leg on a rock—and quickly fell prey to infections and malaria. Knowing he would become a burden to the expedition and further risk the men's lives, Roosevelt made the decision to end his life, asking the men to leave him in the jungle. His son, on the expedition at his father's request, refused to go; he would stay with his father and die by his side. Here Teddy Roosevelt's legendary confidence came into play in a positive way. Knowing he could never allow his son to die, Roosevelt reversed his decision (*responsibility*). "There was only one thing for me to do, and that was to come out myself." From that moment forward, Roosevelt put all his energy into survival.

Six weeks into the expedition, the nearly destitute expedition party came upon a settlement of rubber men (settlers who were there to tap the Amazon's rubber trees). This was their salvation. Although they were still fifteen days from true civilization, Roosevelt and his company finally had access to provisions and people with knowledge of the terrain.

Two weeks later, the expedition ended. Of the nineteen men who had set out, sixteen returned. Roosevelt had lost fifty-five pounds and spent several weeks on bed rest. He returned to the United States to lead a triumphant speaking tour but would never fully recover from the strain of the journey. After everything he had survived, Roosevelt died in 1919 from health complications from his sojourn along the River of Doubt.

Another father-son excursion that illustrates the dangers of being overconfident is one I know far more upfront and personally. In the epilogue you'll read more about my seventy-nine-year-old father's ascent with me of Mount Kilimanjaro in June 2014. My father held to a spiritual belief that he would make it, so he didn't worry when things went awry. He was so sure in his success that when we initially met to discuss the trip, I decided to impress the seriousness of the climb by describing all the ways it could go horribly wrong—even saying that if things got really bad, the price could be *his life*.

When I finished my speech, I was sure I had scared him off. He looked at me for a moment and then told me we had one more important point to discuss. I was ready for the inevitable resignation to reality. Instead, he went on to say, seriously, "Given that you have suffered from altitude sickness one time before on a ski trip, if it were to happen again on our climb, am I free to leave you behind if you can't make the summit?"

I about fell out of my chair. This—combined with his telling me, "I won't make any contingency plans, just preventative ones."—was overconfidence plain and simple. Had he heard anything I said? (Disclaimer: Given that he summited the mountain and returned in one piece, perhaps he was right to have been so assured. Fortunately, he backed up his confidence by building a loyal team of people, like the mountain guides, to look out for him during the climb.)

Danger #2: Underestimating the Unknown

Beyond sheer hubris, Roosevelt also demonstrated a disastrous tendency to underestimate factors that were beyond the expedition party's control. From heat and rain to jaguars to the strength of the river itself, the group walked themselves into disaster. This is not an uncommon tendency, particularly in the outdoors. Inexperienced people underestimate factors like weather or rough terrain because they don't know any better; experienced hikers do so when they believe too strongly in their own capabilities to overcome them.

People chronically underestimate the force external factors can exert. Sometimes the decision is a short-term one, like choosing to drive on icy roads at night. At other times, it is a series of decisions over a long period of time, like not taking proper care of our health until we are faced with a heart attack or diabetes. Misplaced confidence isn't confidence; it is denial or arrogance about our abilities. We start to believe something could *never* happen to us, so we don't prepare. Or, we have an overinflated sense of our own abilities and end up gambling at much higher stakes than we intended to.

Having a good handle on your overconfidence can save your life (literally or figuratively). I see this in business scenarios all the time. Over-optimism, without enough logical support, leads to the overwhelming rate of failures in the corporate world. Isn't this what happens with many failed marriages as well? Letting emotions rule, logic goes out to lunch. Never gamble when the number of uncontrolled factors is too high, whether it is with your money, your relationships, or your life.

Danger #3: Trusting Historical Outcomes

We rely on our experiences to help us predict the future. (Remember those mental models that predicted whether or not we would find snakes on our pleasant hike?) This is an incredibly useful trait, one we rely on constantly as we navigate our daily lives. But when circumstances change and we continue to view them based on our old models about how the world works, we end up in trouble.

Nowhere is this more dramatic than with hurricanes. Oftentimes the victims had ample time to evacuate but they chose not to because they had survived prior hurricanes. They came to believe their homes and selves were indestructible. Circumstances change quickly, especially in extreme survival scenarios. One tropical storm is not like another. While you should place value in your experiences, you have to remain attuned to the present. Treat every decision as a new one that requires its own analysis. This kind of vigilance is key.

Complacency is a killer in survival scenarios. I can fly from Cleveland to Chicago five times in a week, but I am making a different flight every time: The clouds and ceilings are different; the wind is different. I have to refigure wind correction angles and course corrections every time. I can't use the same patterns because there are dynamic forces at play. Thunderstorms, traffic patterns, obstacles like cranes or closed runways—these factors mean that every flight is *totally different*. And I certainly can't "remake" a decision that results in disaster if I've flown according to the previous flight plan with old information that no longer applies.

Interestingly, complacency becomes the biggest problem when you have enough experience to feel confident but not enough to have mastered a skill. For example, most aviation accidents take place when a pilot has around 1,000 hours of flying experience. The 1,000-hour mark is considered nearly as risky as the 100-hour mark. With every 100-hour block of experience new pilots gain, they keep building more confidence and pushing the boundaries. It's at those milestones that pilots have just enough successes to believe they are invincible.

Overconfidence holds true in sports as well. Coaches spend a lot of time telling teams that their twenty-fourth game is just as critical as their first game was, no matter what their record. They point to the New England Patriots as a classic example. They went 16 and 0 in the regular season in 2007 then lost the championship against the New York Giants in Super Bowl XLII. How many promising young athletes flame out early because they become overconfident about their abilities and then don't keep up with their hardworking peers?

THE FINE LINE: AWARENESS AND PREPARATION ARE HEALTHY

It's clearly dangerous to have too much confidence, but you also can't afford to have too little. So how much is enough?

I believe that *true confidence* is a mixture of an unshakable confidence in yourself, a healthy awareness of how many factors are outside your control, and a recognition of just how quickly circumstances can change. It sounds neurotic, but it isn't. Staying confident but vigilant is how you survive. In *Only the Paranoid Survive*, former Intel CEO Andy Grove applies this advice to businesses: watch for strategic inflection points when something like the competition or technological advances change the rules of the game. Such wise counsel, published in the nineties, still has relevance today.

In my company we've recently made changes to our core business that will, we hope, reflect a predicted inflection point. Population growth in Ohio has flatlined, and its citizens are aging. Instead of continuing to focus our investments in office spaces or hotels, we have decided to make senior living communities our bread and butter. By making the change now, we are getting ahead of the market rather than sitting complacently.

The Naysayers

An interesting mutation of confidence is the drive we get to prove the naysayers wrong. (Reflect for a moment on Teddy Roosevelt's instant rejection of those who cautioned against the Amazon expedition.) How often are we told we can't do something? We don't have the proper qualifications or skills, or luck isn't on our side. Sometimes this comes in the form of well-meant advice to do a "reality check," but the feedback still feels crushing. Our reaction can be to capitulate to the negativity—or to nurture a sense of healthy defiance.

I see healthy defiance in many people I admire. Wade Hoag nails it when he says he both accepts his new situation ("I'm in a wheelchair") while also totally rejecting the limitations being in a wheelchair has put on him. Similarly, my sister-in-law, Rhonda, who is in her fifties and raising two young daughters, is putting herself through college. I asked her why she was so intent on pursuing her degree now amid so many obstacles.

"Because someone told me I couldn't do it," she said with a gleam in her eye. "My very first class, the professor came to me and said there was no way, given how long I'd been out of school and my situation, that I'd make it through the class. I'm here to prove her wrong." It was so funny hearing this out-for-blood attitude from Rhonda, one of the sweetest people I know.

I empathize with what Rhonda feels. When I got into

real estate investing, I brought my uncle, a man I admired and thought of as a mentor, to see the very first house I'd bought. He'd always been very supportive of me, but he took one look at that house and said, "Oh my god, you've just made the biggest mistake of your life." That appraisal motivated me just as much as anything encouraging he said. I have realized that almost all my business deals follow this pattern. Second-guessers chime in with unsolicited "advice," and suddenly I become even more interested in pursuing deals where others can't see the opportunity.

Oftentimes, you're motivated more by the words of an authority figure who tells you you're going to fail ("Your idea is flawed. You will never succeed.") than you are by the words of someone who tells you you're going to be great. "Healthy defiance has fueled many successes. Will this be the beginning or the end of your success? You decide.

Even When It Seems Hopeless . . .

In many of the survival stories you've read about thus far, the odds have been stacked against the survivor. Indeed, there can be moments in a survival journey when continuing on seems hopeless. Why keep struggling if your efforts won't matter?

This is when having confidence in your plan is key. Deciding to carry on and continue investing in your plan when the chances of survival are slim requires tremendous discipline and confidence in yourself. You have to believe that your plan has a solid chance of leading to your survival. You have to believe that your life is worth it. And you have to believe that you're tough enough to keep going. The only way you get here is by committing to your survival and taking it one moment at a time.

An example of a man who confidently stuck with his survival

plan when all odds seemed against him is Harrison Okene.[13] The twenty-nine-year-old Nigerian sailor was a cook on board the tugboat *Jacson 4*. Early in the morning of May 26, 2013, the tugboat was hit by a rogue wave and capsized. Harrison was already awake for his shift when he felt the boat go over. He watched helplessly as several crewmembers were washed away; he was swept into one of the bathrooms and grabbed onto a sink to keep from being sucked from the boat. The boat quickly sank ninety feet to the ocean floor.

Miraculously, an air bubble formed in the ship's hull just as it capsized. Harrison found himself in this air bubble, able to wade from room to room in the dark. Groping through the cabins, he discovered a life vest and two emergency beacons, plus one can of Coke. He lit one of the beacons and used it to guide him through the ship to a mostly dry cabin. Using pieces of the wall and a mattress, he made himself a small platform to stand on in the cabin. He watched the water continue to rise—and sighed when it stopped at chest height.

Harrison was now trapped in a truly hellish scenario. He was living in the air bubble, hoping that the oxygen in the cramped space would not run out. His body was partially submerged in the water, and he could hear sharks swimming around the sunken ship, devouring the bodies of his dead companions. He had no food and no potable water; that one can of Coke would have to sustain him.

He also had no idea whether people were coming for him.

So he made a plan: stay calm, wait (*evaluation*). Panicking would have further diminished his air supply in the four-foot

---

13 Kenneth Miller, "Drama in Real Life: Trapped on the Bottom of the Ocean," *Reader's Digest*, July 2014.

high pocket. Attempting to swim through the ship was also too dangerous. He also could not cut his way through the steel hull. Harrison began passing the time by praying and also reliving his life story, trying to concentrate on happy moments. He refused to sleep, afraid of sharks finding him and attacking the submerged lower half of his body. Eventually the emergency beacons ran out, and he was left in utter darkness. Still he neither slept nor panicked, continuing to pray and to wait. This was the only thing he could do if he wanted to be found alive.

Harrison spent a total of nearly sixty hours trapped in the overturned tugboat at the bottom of the sea. Rescue divers—sent to retrieve bodies and check out the ship for insurance purposes—found him when they knocked on the hull. They were shocked to hear an answering knock. They put an oxygen mask on Harrison and swam him to the surface where he spent sixty hours (the equivalent of the time he had been underwater) in a decompression chamber. He also required medical attention for hypothermia and for his skin, which had peeled after being soaked in saltwater for sixty hours. Harrison was the only one to survive the accident. Not surprisingly, Okene admitted he made a pact with God when he was trapped at the bottom of the ocean. "When I was under the water I told God: 'If you rescue me, I will never go back to the sea again, never.'"

Another sole survivor of tragedy was invited by my YPO group to describe his experience. Beck Weathers was high on Mount Everest in May 1996 when a blizzard stuck, effectively stranding his entire party near the summit. The timing was bad, but for Beck it couldn't have been worse: he'd simultaneously been struck with temporary blindness due to the altitude and exposure.

Beck was "left for dead on Everest" (the title of his memoir) and survived only because he forced himself to walk down the mountain in the midst of the storm. He couldn't see, so he judged his position by leaning into the direction of the wind, which he assumed was blowing up the mountain. This was an excellent *evaluation* of his changing circumstances that ended up saving his life. He took *action* and staggered into camp hours later.

The men in my group were highly impressed by Beck's speech on resilience. He survived a true nightmare and paid for it with several amputations (right forearm, left-hand fingers, and nose). He survived because he *decided* he was going to, for his family and for himself. (His testimony echoes the motivation expressed by the survivors you read about in chapter 1 in the section "Declare Your Dependents," of course.)

My friends and I thought he was a real badass. We turned to our wives and discovered they'd had a totally opposite reaction. Leaving his wife and infant for most of the year to train, travel, and risk his life? What a jerk.

Executing your survival plan with confidence is the mark of a survivor. You don't have the luxury of questioning or mistrusting yourself. Every survivor in the scenarios above stuck with their plan; their confidence translated itself into tenacity. Their situations seemed hopeless, but they had confidence that their plans could lead to a way out of the situation they were in.

Some people are confident because they are prepared; past experiences have shown them to be a survivor. Others have a confidence that comes almost from desperation; they need to survive, for themselves or for others, and their plan is their best bet. Some survivors have a faith in themselves or something bigger that is innate. Regardless, everyone finds and strengthens their confidence by committing to a survival plan. The small wins incrementally build your confidence in yourself, but you have to commit to taking the first step.

For some people their confidence in survival is like a calling: "This is what I was made for." They pay little attention to the predicted outcomes, that is, what people were telling them their fate might be. The thought of death was present, but their survival journey became the focus. They found peace in that calling. For survivors, it's a matter of finding the eye at the center of the storm. You can't control the storm around you, but you need to find the calm center and focus on the task at hand.

Having confidence doesn't mean you aren't willing to let your survival plan change. Remember, part of the *evaluation* element in REACH is continuing to assess and analyze at every stage of the journey. Stefani Schaefer (chapter 1), whose husband suffered a traumatic brain injury, explains that choices she made about how to handle the situation or her son and daughter early in their survival journey she would not make now. Just because she has had to refine her plan doesn't mean she has lost confidence in her ability to make decisions. It is a learning process. As Nando Parrado put it, his life was a perfect book until you got to chapter 8; thereafter, he'd had rewrite chapters 9 through 12. Stefani might say the same thing; she is rewriting chapters all the time, but that doesn't mean the book won't be better for it—or that she's spent any time second-guessing the earlier decisions she made.

Confident people are open to reevaluating their plan. They know when to tap community resources and ask for help. They are realistic about their abilities and the influence external factors can have on their plans. Confident people have faith that they can make it, without blaming themselves when factors out of their control wreck their plans. Having confidence in your plan and in yourself is the only way to find some level of peace on your survival journey.

Understand that there is little clarity in survival. In most of these situations, the only factor that is evident to the person involved is that something must be done. Many times having a plan can be as simple as refusing to stay where you are, and pushing yourself into a new direction. Confidence is just the decision to keep moving forward no matter what.

CHAPTER 5

HAPPINESS

Recovering from five shots to various body parts is not an experi-
ence most of us will ever have. Neither, thankfully, is living with the
memories of defending fellow students against an unstable man who
terrorized the campus, killing nine others and wounding at least that
many more. It would seem like Chris Mintz doesn't have much to be
grateful for, but he doesn't always see it that way.

While he's fairly quiet in the media, his Facebook page is awash
with uplifting and empowering sentiments: messages of gratitude for
people who have donated to his medical care or the care of other shoot-
ing victim; pictures of his son; updates about his physical health—for
example, five months after the attack and many surgeries, Chris was
able to run his first mile; even gym selfies showing off his fitness.

One of the photos he added about a month after the accident is
a picture of him sitting in his car, with a big grin on his face. The
caption reads: "Some days you just gotta smile through the sadness."

I want to be careful how I discuss our final element, *happiness*. Without the right context, it sounds naive or even cruel to advise you to "be happy" if you're in the middle of fighting for your life.

Many people don't associate happiness and survival. *Responsibility, evaluation, action, confidence*—these all seem like a natural fit for a true survival outlook. But happiness? Does it sound like I've gone very New Age on you?

We wouldn't imagine someone down in the trenches of survival being happy; rather, we would expect them to be tough or serious. This is because many people tend to think about happiness as just laughter or smiling. In the REACH protocol, however, I define *being happy* as holding onto hope and finding moments of joy even when the struggle becomes dark. The use of the word "happiness" is, in many ways, symbolic for *positivity* and *hope*.

People derive happiness in their survival journeys in different ways. Particularly in extreme or isolated survival situations, maintaining positivity becomes a matter of appreciating the beauty of your surroundings. Survivors stuck in Arctic ice, on life rafts in the Pacific, or in the middle of the jungle all report being awestruck by nature. Noticing this beauty pulled them out of a narrow—and potentially enervating—focus on their suffering.

In other scenarios, especially when there is more than one person in the survival situation, happiness comes from community. Being able to positively relate to the people around you who can empathize with your situation is key. The opposite is also true. When communication and respect break down, survival becomes infinitely more difficult.

As I was writing this book I had some doubts about whether this element was really *happiness* when *hope* seemed like an equally good choice. Although hope is critical, it isn't enough. You must act. And when you do, happiness is the result. I'm reminded of these sage words of writer J. K. Rowling: "Happiness can be found in the darkest of times, if only one remembers to turn the light on."

And, echoing my earlier writings about spirituality, it's not enough to have faith; you must act on it. Hope and faith translated into action yield the energy-rich state of happiness.

If you think about your favorite epic survival story, I have no doubt it features a survivor who relied on positive thinking. Someone who believed they would make it and appreciated their life even when ugliness was all around them. The stories in this chapter will be no different, featuring survivors of POW camps, being stranded at sea, a plane crash, cancer, and poverty—each of whom found happiness even when the odds were against them. Happiness for them meant appreciation, hope, living in the moment, gratitude—anything that broke the cycle of negative thinking and got them focused on the positive outcome of survival.

The Value of Positivity in Survival

Every person has his or her own definition of what "happiness" means. What many people don't know is that there is a science behind happiness and positive thinking. For years researchers in fields like psychology and behavioral economics have worked to define what happiness is and why it is important in all areas of our lives, from personal satisfaction to business.

There is even research proving that positivity is linked to mortality. In his book *Chasing Life*, for instance, Dr. Sanjay Gupta writes about a study of 660 individuals that was undertaken in 2002.[14] Those deemed to have a positive outlook on themselves and aging increased their longevity by 7.5 years compared with respondents who had a "poor" outlook. In other words, in terms of long-term survival, you will literally live longer if you are positive.

Unfortunately, no comparable studies generalize about positivity and survival scenarios. But, anecdotally, I have never read a survival story that featured a negative survivor as the hero. You don't make it through tough stuff by refusing to accept responsibility, complaining, and resigning yourself to bad outcomes. You don't win if you think that nothing in life is worth fighting for or that there isn't any chance you will make it. Appreciation for what you have is the superhighway to happiness and survival success.

Positive Survivors Choose Happiness

Happiness isn't a state of being but a choice. By embracing positivity you aren't taking the easy way out, you are taking *action*, especially when you are totally limited by your circumstances and, as Viktor Frankl teaches, all you can control is how you feel. As author Stephen Covey puts it: "Sometimes the most proactive thing we can do is to *be* happy, just to genuinely smile. Happiness, like unhappiness, is a proactive choice."[15]

Remember that you don't have to be on a life raft two thousand miles from shore to appreciate the value of positive

---

14 Gupta cited Levy, Slade, Kunkel, and Kasl's "Longevity Increased by Positive Self-Perceptions of Aging" (New Haven: *Journal of Personality and Social Psychology*, 2002).

15 Stephen R. Covey, *The 7 Habits of Highly Effective People* (New York: Simon & Schuster, 2004), 90.

thinking in hard times; positivity is a tool in everyday incidents and interactions as well.

Once again I'm reminded of my friend Rick, whose son died in a car accident (you heard part of their story in chapter 1). Rick is encouraged to share stories about Alex—athletic, intelligent, sharply funny, and quietly confident—as part of his therapy. What people remember most about Alex-beyond his achievements, is his character. For example, Alex stopped playing lacrosse during high school because his goal was to play Division 1 basketball. His senior year, he emailed the coach to ask if he could be brought back on the lacrosse team halfway through the season. Alex didn't expect playing time; he just wanted to spend time with the guys and add to team morale however he could.

The coach, very touched, said yes. As painful as it is to dwell on how much has been lost, it helps Rick to remember what a remarkable young man Alex was.

At the one-year anniversary of their deaths in the car crash, the SMAC, an AAU Basketball League Alex played for, high school sponsored a memorial basketball tournament called "Catch Me If You Can" in his honor. Thousands of young hoopers attended the three-day event, inspired by Alex's legacy.

Rick says that he knows that if Alex were given a choice on that fateful day of who would survive and who would die, he would have chosen himself without hesitation. "He was just that kind of kid—brave, humble, kind, unique . . ." Rick says, "His family and friends were everything to him."

Alex doing what he loved most.

I got to enjoy some time with Rick this last fall at his house on Lake Walloon, where he and Alex spent lots of time. It was tough getting back into Alex's ski boat, but Rick jumped in. I think, in many ways, he keeps going because he knows he has Alex's legacy to uphold.

As Rick says, "There's still a lot to celebrate. Alex was a model for good character that needs to be shared. I am grateful for his inspiration and impact every day. As painful as it is to share, it is more important for us to remember and be reminded of the important things in life and how fragile it is. As painful as it all still is, I would never give up how wonderful the last eighteen years have been."

Alex Doody

Positivity and Resilience Go Hand in Hand

Positivity is at the core of resilience. According to the work of Stanford University psychologist Carol Dweck, as laid out in her book *Mindset,* positive people have what's called a "growth mindset"—that is, they don't believe failure is a permanent condition. Every hardship becomes an opportunity for growth, not a stopping point.

You'll learn more about Colonel Lee Ellis, US Air Force, retired later in this chapter, but I want to share his reflections on positivity at this point in the discussion of the REACH protocol. Lee holds one philosophy in particular that has truly served him well. He believes that, fundamentally, life is difficult. The sooner you accept that life is a tumultuous journey, the easier you'll have it because you'll do the hard work of defining who you are, what you stand for, and why you need to keep going. Lee is a man who knows what he stands for. His commitment to his mission, fellow servicemen, and country saved both his integrity and his life in ways that most of us will never experience.

This quote from Lee's memoir, *Leading with Honor*, sums up his "formula" for resilience. I think you might find it familiar: "A strong will and a positive outlook, undergirded by an unwavering commitment to duty, can overcome enormous hardships. Add to that the support of others and a strong spiritual faith, and you have the fundamental formula for bouncing back."

I would add another element to that formula. It's what University of Pennsylvania psychology professor Angela Duckworth calls grit—a combination of perseverance and passion over the long run. And, according to her research, high achievers show a lot of it. It seems that older adults naturally have more grit than younger people do.[16]

Grit isn't about intelligence or talent. It is about the belief that your challenges—even if you screw up—can't sink you.[17] In other words, hope. This is the kind of positivity survivors cultivate. It is a special kind of happiness.

The call to positivity in survival is a double-edged sword.

---

16 Lois A. Bowers, "Combating aging perceptions with aging realities," *McKnight's Senior Living*, November 7, 2016. www.mcknightseniorliving.com.

17 Angela Duckworth, Ph.D., "The Key to Success? Grit" TED Talk, May 2013.

Finding happiness, akin to taking responsibility, requires acceptance of your circumstances; your old life is over and you're on a new path. There is no turning back the clock. The pain is real. Now you're in it. At a certain point it becomes a matter of radical acceptance: "I won't let this experience take anything else from me."

Remember the DePenti family I introduced you to in chapter 1? Part two of their survival story exemplifies the positivity (as well as giving back) that Stefani strives for as she and her son and daughter conduct their lives in ways that honor an absent husband and father who no longer recognizes them.

The family's life now does not look like it did in the months following Roger's tragic accident; some of the hopelessness and panic have abated. Being able to slowly have more control in shaping her children's daily lives was a critical choice Stefani made.

"The way we are getting through this is by being positive. In a perfect world, I wish there was total healing. But talking to doctors and experts, I know that won't happen. Our miracle was that Roger survived. In five years, I want to see Race and Siena continue to be faith-filled, thriving, happy, and empathetic young people. We've been able to raise a lot of money for traumatic brain injury services . . . and would like to see more research done, so people can have an even better outcome. I would love to continue to help in that fight."

Every year, Stefani hosts the FOX 8 Foxtrot where all the proceeds go to a worthwhile charity. The first year, all the money raised went to the Cleveland's MetroHealth Trauma Center for brain injury research. And she continues to break records every year. Stefani and her kids can be seen everywhere on the Cleveland charity scene, volunteering for nonprofit fundraising events almost every weekend. Despite what has been taken from them, their giving never ends.

Stefani and her children could have had a much different journey after Roger's accident, but she chose a life of generosity, achievement, and love for her family. It's a testament to their love for each—and especially for Roger—that they are such graceful survivors.

The Stockdale Paradox

Stefani Schaefer's type of balanced thinking is best explained by what is referred to as the Stockdale Paradox, first described by Jim Collins in his book *Good to Great*. James Stockdale was a fighter pilot shot down in an early campaign in the Vietnam War. (He was captured and held as a prisoner of war from 1965 to 1973 in the same camp as Lee Ellis, who I mentioned above.)

These eight years were a dark and brutal time. Stockdale was tortured repeatedly. His hands were tied behind his back to cut off circulation. Bones were broken and rebroken. All in pursuit of making Stockdale sign confessions lambasting the US government and supporting the Communist regime in Vietnam.

Stockdale didn't know when he would be released. He wasn't allowed any contact with his family. Technically, he wasn't even allowed contact with the other prisoners in the jail. As one of the ranking officers in the camp, however, he fought to figure out ways to keep the men's spirits up. To foster resilience and community through covert communication and discipline. Stockdale himself "never doubted not only that I would get out, but also that I would prevail in the end and turn the experience into *the defining event of my life*, which, in retrospect, I would not trade." It's little wonder, then, why Ellis remembers Stockdale as a giant in the camp, someone he relied on for guidance and strength.

When asked about who didn't make it through imprisonment at the Hanoi Hilton, Stockdale had a quick answer: "The optimists."

Jim Collins, who was interviewing him, was utterly confused.

Pressed further, Stockdale explained that there's a difference between blind optimism and optimistic realism. An optimistic realist focuses on *changing their mindset* rather than their external, uncontrollable circumstances. They focus on the result they want (being released from prison with their honor intact) rather than *when* they will get the result they want. In the meantime, they are honest with themselves about their circumstances in the present moment.

For example, Stockdale explained that the prisoners who believed that they would be out by Christmas would end up crushed when December 25 rolled around and they were still in leg irons. Stockdale believed that they would *someday* get out, but he consciously didn't set himself up for disappointment; therefore, he made plans for their time that went beyond deadlines.

Collins condensed the Stockdale Paradox into these words:

> *You must retain faith that you will prevail in the end, regardless of the difficulties.*
>
> *AND at the same time . . .*
>
> *You must confront the most brutal facts of your current reality, whatever they might be.*

Thank goodness most of us won't see the inside of a North Vietnamese POW camp. Nevertheless, all of us come to a moment where we face the choice of how we handle the pain of survival. For Wade Hoag, it was when his girlfriend broke up with him, saying she couldn't be with anyone in a wheelchair.

"I decided right then that I wouldn't let this take anything else from me. In that moment of excruciating pain and anguish, I found peace and a sort of twisted happiness. Freedom is what you do with what has been done to you. Confidence is knowing that no matter what is done to you, you'll do something good with it."

Happiness and Confidence Have a Symbiotic Relationship

Even better than Wade's inspiring comment is the reality that *happiness* has a fundamental connection to the "C" element in REACH, *confidence*. Feeling certain, whether that's in your choices or the path ahead of you, could release dopamine in your brain as you experience the "pleasure of being right."[18] Dopamine is also known as the "happiness hormone." In other words, chemically speaking, confidence equals happiness! That positivity that comes from your conviction in your choices and yourself is the kind of *happiness* that is relevant to survival.

In chapter 1 I quoted Lee Ellis's sage comments about forgiveness as a key part of surviving the unspeakable. Lee spent five years as a POW in the Vietnam War. At any given moment, he said, the American prisoners could have easily become despondent and overwhelmed by thoughts of never seeing their

---

18 Robert A. Burton, M.D., *On Being Certain: Believing You Are Right Even When You're Not* (St. Martin's Griffin, 2009), 97–100.

families again, by losing their fellow inmates on a regular basis. Their manipulated minds were weakening. Their beaten bodies were wavering. They wanted to escape not only their walls but their very skin as well.

Fighting through what Lee calls an "army of oppressive feelings" every day—fear, anger, disappointment, and guilt— was at the core of their inner struggle, never mind the external pressures they faced. But the POWs were highly motivated to survive and uphold their integrity. As military leaders, they were "trained to make the best of a situation by solving problems rather than stewing about them" (*action*), and as fighter pilots, who are inherently confident people, they were trained to visualize the success they wanted. So they organized. Covert communications were established all over the camp, from using a 5x5 matrix tapping code to sign language. Being able to communicate rallied the men as a community, enabled an effective chain of command, and added to their ability to resist their captors.

Lee explains that rebelling against the North Vietnamese was key to survival. Whether that resistance took the form of refusing to sign pro-Communist statements, being rude to their jailers, or "devious tricks," their ability to fight back strengthened their belief in themselves and their integrity. "As we settled into this new life, we gained *confidence* we would survive." That confidence fueled their hopefulness given how bleak their circumstances seemed. As Lee puts it, "Maintaining a *positive* outlook was crucial for survival."

Lee Ellis

That positive outlook wasn't just necessary for the interrogation room. According to Lee, their experience was one of boredom punctuated by moments of terror. The years of long hours trapped in a cell were torturous in their own way. The men found different ways of enduring their imprisonment. For example, some of the more restless men "hiked" around their cell, doing miles and miles of laps to keep themselves in shape and to give their frenetic energy an outlet.

Find the Beauty

When I first began my research into survival stories, I was shocked by how positive people managed to be when stuck in the worst situations. The first story that drove this point home for me was Louis Zamperini's, as relayed in Lauren Hillenbrand's *Unbroken: A World War II Story of Survival, Resilience, and Redemption*. Throughout every one of his ordeals—the plane crash, being stranded at sea, being sent to a POW camp—Zamperini never lost hope. He was always coming up with a plan, drawing together the other soldiers, and staying focused on the possibility of a brighter future.

Part of Zamperini's ability to stay positive while adrift was based upon a mindset that enabled him to appreciate the beauty of the ocean around them. Shockingly, this is a theme in almost all "shipwrecked" scenarios. Zamperini's sixty-three days at sea were impressive enough, but another man, Salvador Alvarenga, spent an *additional three hundred and seventy-six days* at sea— and used the same positive mindset to survive.[19]

It was the middle of November. Salvador Alvarenga, an El Salvadorian, was captaining a fishing boat fifty miles off Mexico when a powerful storm struck. An experienced fisherman, Alvarenga knew how to run massive waves in a small fishing boat. His companion for the day, however, a young man named

---

19 Jonathan Franklin, "Lost at Sea: the Man Who Vanished for 14 Months," *The Guardian*, November 7, 2015.

Ezequiel Cordoba, did not. He had picked up the shift on a whim when Alvarenga invited him to replace his regular partner. The consequences of bringing an inexperienced sailor on board were serious. As the storm conditions worsened, Cordoba began to panic. Alvarenga was left to steer the ship and bail water on his own until he could calm Cordoba down.

Their bad day making a run for shore in rough surf would turn into a disaster of unthinkable proportions. Still a fair distance out to sea, the boat's engine died. Alvarenga had no way to negotiate the waves or get back to Mexico. He radioed in an SOS call and was instructed to relay his GPS coordinates and put down an anchor. Both were impossible; his GPS wasn't working and he didn't have an anchor. There was nothing Alvarenga or his would-be rescuers could do. The men were swept out to sea.

The two fishermen began a serious fight for their survival. With the water they were taking on, the boat—laden with heavy equipment and a morning's worth of fish—was in danger of capsizing. Rather than sleep, the two men spent every moment their muscles could bear bailing water out of the boat.

Alvarenga began throwing out their day's catch and then the equipment in order to lighten the boat's load. This undoubtedly saved their lives for the moment but, long-term, had critical implications. They were left with almost nothing apart from an empty refrigerator, buckets, a knife, and a few other odds and ends.

The men started to fish with their bare hands and also scavenged from the ocean, picking out useful trash (plastic bottles) and food (rotten cabbages and milk) that floated by. Alvarenga created a "rainwater collection system" in anticipation of a gentler storm. His planning (*evaluation*) paid off. After two weeks passed, it rained and the men had copious water supplies thanks to Alvarenga's system. The two men celebrated—and then put themselves on a strict rationing plan.

As the days went on, the men fell into a routine and established a backup food supply. Feeling a little more secure with both in place, they "found solace in the magnificent seascape." The beauty around them inspired deep discussions about family and what they would do if given a second chance.

For Alvarenga, their functioning plan, the beauty of the sea, and their philosophical conversations sustained him. Cordoba, on the other hand, began to sink into a depression. First he refused food. Then water. Despite begging him to fight on, Alvarenga's support did not have any effect. Cordoba died within days.

Alvarenga was determined to live. Even without Cordoba, he still stuck to his routine: fishing, watching for ships. The chances of a ship spotting his tiny craft were slim, but he kept his vigil. He shares that every ship sighting, although ultimately futile, gave him an extra energy boost that kept him going. (His experience was not unlike that described in "The Stockdale Paradox" previously.)

He also began to use his imagination, living a vibrant interior life while trapped on the boat. In an interview with the *Guardian*, he shared that "alone at sea he tasted the greatest meals of his life and experienced the most delicious sex"—all in his mind. This is how he came to sustain himself alone in the boat.

Four hundred and thirty-eight days after he had left the shores of Mexico, Alvarenga washed up on the shores of Tile Islet in the Marshall Islands. He had traveled 6,700 miles.

Alvarenga's survival journey is a remarkable one; so remarkable, in fact, that many people believed it to be fabricated. An investigation proved, inasmuch as it can, that the fisherman is telling the truth. He arrived in the Marshalls in the same boat he'd set out in and could medically be described only as someone who had spent a long, long time at sea.

The most striking element of his story to me is his continued effort to be hopeful and to find joy. The man spent more than a year alone in a 25-foot boat eating raw birds and turtles and yet still used his imagination to create the "best" experiences of his life. He also found the ocean beautiful. The kind of resilience required to make this journey undoubtedly came from positivity.

It is not just sailors adrift at sea who find beauty in their surroundings. In 1992, Annette Herfkens was on a Vietnam Airlines flight from Tan Son Nhat to Nha Trang with her fiancé, Pasje. On approach to the Nha Trang airport, the plane dropped too low and clipped some trees, causing it to crash into a ridge at around 300 mph.[20] Herfkens felt the plummeting and remembers the plane rolling down the mountain before she blacked out. "I woke up and everyone was dead."[21]

While not dead, Herfkens was in bad shape. Her entire body had been battered in the crash. Even worse, her leg was broken; she could tell because four inches of bone were sticking out of her shin. It would have been easy, faced with her dead fiancé and twenty-nine other corpses around her, to give up. But Herfkens did not.

"I got real," she related—that is, accepting *responsibility*. Her options in terms of plans were limited, seeing as she was unable

---

20   Jeff Wise, "The Gift and the Guilt of Sole Survivors," *Reader's Digest*, 2014.

21   Jordan Chittley, "Sole plane crash survivor lives eight days on rain water," *CTV News*, March 28, 2014.

to walk, but she dragged herself from the wreckage—and waited. She had no food or water, so if it rained, she would squeeze water into her mouth from her clothes or pieces of the aircraft.

What kept her alive was her refusal to fall into despair. "I managed to focus on the beauty of the jungle," she explains. "I was one with the beauty and process of decay around me." She spent eight days in the jungle covered in leeches, her body slowly shutting down, before help finally came.

An upside of slowing down and taking a moment to appreciate natural beauty is that you place yourself in a larger context. Your struggles suddenly aren't the dominant force at play. This is true in everyday survival as well. If you are able to bring yourself outside your suffering and appreciate the beauty around you, you might gain some perspective on your struggles. At the very least, you will find a brief respite from the harshness of some of life's realities, as Herfkens did.

Interestingly, Herfkens revisited Vietnam in 2006, including trekking to the crash site that she remembered as being so beautiful, verdant and green and framed by towering mountains. What she found shocked her. "It was so much more claustrophobic than I remembered. And not as green. And not as pretty."

Herfkens's second trip provides interesting insight into finding beauty in survival scenarios. Viewed objectively from outside a survival scenario, the jungle was not pretty. It was her positive mindset in the middle of a tragedy that made it so. This might read as a truism, but beauty is about perception. You create beauty for yourself.

When times are dark, being able to find the beauty is an important skill or discipline, not a superficial one. Beauty reminds us that not everything is an ugly fight for survival. Beauty reminds us that there is hope, something to keep fighting for. For example, Viktor Frankl and some of his fellow prisoners would celebrate the sunset as a marker that they had survived another day. They truly experienced a sense of triumph, of healthy rebellion, for surviving another day. For cheating death. For refusing to bow under the insane pressure the Nazi death camps put on them.

Here again I want to stress that their reaction in those camps was not about hope or hopefulness. These men weren't looking to the future as the sun set and they celebrated having lived another day. They found *happiness in that moment*, a happiness that would carry them through the night into another hellish day. There was no guarantee of survival or tomorrow. There was only the joy in the moment of having defied the Nazis' murderous intent and made it through once more.

Solace in Companionship

Not every survival journey is a solo journey. You might have companions in your own survival scenario. This is a blessing and a curse. Other people can either be invaluable strategic resources and sources of comfort or a terrible drain.

I am sure by now you realize that all people respond to survival situations in their own way. When you find yourself in a survival scenario, there is no guarantee that you will end up with a resilient companion. When things get rough, people tend to surprise you—for better or worse.

I learned this lesson the hard way in the 2008-2009 Great Recession. My industry was hit especially hard. The national banking crisis and near collapse of the financial system as we knew it caused plummeting real estate values in all categories. Multimillion-dollar portfolios that were thought to be invincible and conservative lost 50 percent to 70 percent of their value overnight.

Wall Street demanded that banks purge their commercial real estate loan portfolios in whatever manner provided the most efficient exit, even if that meant going on the offensive against their borrowers and longtime clientele. Thousands of jobs lost because of the collapse of entities like Lehman Brothers caused the edgy bankers to sharpen their teeth in the process; otherwise, their jobs were next.

The toxicity in the business environment was pervasive and fostered an "eat or be eaten" mentality. Midsize developers and owners with formerly healthy balance sheets were placed in the crosshairs of the frenetic and desperate banks and financial institutions. More than $50 million in judgment liens were immediately filed against me in an effort to preempt my ex-wife's position in claiming any scraps that remained. The twelve bank lawyers who showed up at the court on the first day of my divorce trial would further underscore the seriousness of my situation.

How would I ever dig out? How would I get a divorce without the money to pay the nine attorneys between us? How would I attempt to pay mortgages with fifty-two financial restraining orders bearing down on our company in an effort to extort an advantageous and unbalanced settlement?

When banks began calling back real estate loans, my partner and I approached our passive investors in the hopes that we could work together to pull the businesses through. Only about 10 percent stepped up to the plate. The other 90 percent either pointed fingers or turned tail and ran. I was devastated.

But all it takes is one person who is willing to stand by you in very dark times to prove that humanity isn't a waste. For me it was my partner, Doug Leohr.

Doug and I met in a college real estate investment class. Our first partnership started almost immediately thereafter. We shared a thirst for entrepreneurship and a common desire to be independent from the corporate bureaucratic jobs popular with new finance college grads. As we built several businesses together, the promise of this independence became more and more achievable.

Twenty years later, with a notable and diversified portfolio, we were now facing the financial crisis. Doug came well equipped to handle those challenges. During the years of the crisis, I witnessed and tried to emulate this master problem-solver. Setting his ego aside, he artfully negotiated with the banks to win many small battles and incremental settlements and solutions. He took the process one step at a time rather than being overwhelmed by the hopelessness of what was happening (*responsibility*).

He was a leader by example and a tactical negotiator. During the painful settlement process, he continued to see opportunity even through all the scorched earth (*evaluation*). The "game" that kept us going was being able to springboard from the few spoils left behind in the form of drastically discounted projects needing a capable developer. In hindsight, these opportunities that Doug highlighted were some of the best in our careers. This became the motivator as we dug ourselves out, one inch at a time.

Little did we know, however, the toxic and stressful environment would take its toll on Doug. A few years into the financial recovery, he discovered he had another battle to fight: Stage 3 colon and bladder cancer. To this day, he attributes the rampant growth of his cancer to the stress and disillusionment of those days. (His oncologist was the first to posit the theory.)

Doug Leohr

Despite the diagnosis, his oncologist was initially optimistic that, because of the early detection, the cancer could be surgically removed without the need for chemotherapy. During a pre-screening appointment, however, a mass was detected in his bladder. Further testing revealed that Doug had a softball-sized tumor in his bladder.

The cancer had spread. The surgery would need to be immediate and followed by an aggressive chemotherapy regiment. The surgery (the first of many) did not go well. Doug's colon was damaged and rendered unusable. The months—that accrued to total two years—that followed included hauling around a colostomy bag, more surgeries, and numerous emergency hospital visits for septic contamination and infections.

At the same time he was suffering life-threatening cancer, his newly transformed construction and development business took off. He was rebuilding, employing more people than ever, building more than ever, and truly enjoying his life. Every one of his friends was amazed at his perseverance, positive outlook, courage, and devotion—much of which he attributes to his wife, Leslie. Doug never gave up or gave in.

The final surgery came and went. He survived . . . and is cancer free.

Despite all he has been through, Doug refers to himself as "one of the lucky ones." He remembers that some people would arrive for their chemo treatments in a taxi, with no family to help or encourage them. He, on the other hand, had a wife who was there with him every step of the way. For Doug, the small wins and Leslie's presence made all the difference in being able to appreciate his life and find some happiness in truly dark times.

For me, having this kind of partner by my side made a huge difference at a truly low point in my life. I wish everyone could be so lucky as to have a Doug Leohr in their lives when times get rough.

Working Together to Solve Problems

When it comes to survival, you will have little control over the actions of others (as I experienced). Survival scenarios, both extreme and everyday, tend to elevate our actions and reactions. So, you need to bear in mind that you will be dealing with people at their extremes while contending with your own affected mindset. Your job during a crisis will be to identify who can be helpful to you and who you should avoid as much as possible.

It is important to advocate for the survival of the whole group (no one left behind), but that doesn't mean you need to tolerate negativity. Negative people are draining. Your life, metaphorically or literally, is at stake. You need people who, at the very least, can contribute to your state of hopefulness.

If you are in close confines and are unable to physically escape someone's negativity, find a way to insulate yourself. Remember that their negativity might not be a reflection of your plan or chances for survival but a confirmation of their personal inability to cope. The best way to stay positive with this kind of negative energy around you is to use the REACH protocol and maintain *confidence* in your plan. You are in charge. You are the leader. If you believe you are headed in the right direction, you have every reason to be hopeful.

This was something I had to remind myself daily when I was going through my divorce battle. While the helicopter crash might be my flashiest survival story, I can tell you which situation took the greatest toll on my resilience reserves. There were days when hope seemed like a foreign concept. The most painful part of the divorce wasn't the tangible losses—my marriage, our family, a sense of control, our financial security—but the violation of trust. The strategies my ex-wife's attorneys employed to get me flustered and angry represented a deep threat to my integrity.

At one point, and this is a matter of public record, she asked for full custody of the kids on the grounds of abuse. This made me physically ill. This allegation was significantly worse than anything that had or has ever happened to me in my life. The only thing that brought me back on top—and this is a form of *positivity*—was holding onto the knowledge that someday no one would think twice about these charges because they knew me and they would know the allegations couldn't be true.

The charges were upsetting for my sons as well, not only because they were so ugly but also because they weren't true. I had broken the news to them about what their mom was alleging in a gentle, matter-of-fact way. I mentioned it because I knew they would hear about it from other people. They would potentially even be brought in for questioning. Fortunately, it never came to that.

Balancing my relationship with my boys with the pressure my ex-wife sometimes put on them was extremely difficult, even after the divorce. She would spend hours interrogating them immediately after I spent time with them. I didn't want to put my kids through that, but I also refused to not see them. So I was careful, and I held out hope that with time the situation would change for the better. I was *confident* that someday we would find equilibrium.

As was vividly shown in the POW stories at the beginning of this chapter, finding joy in grim circumstances is much easier if you can work together with other committed survivors toward survival. This was certainly true for me during my divorce as I relied on the love of my family and Gina and trusted friends to help me work through the situation. A bonus is that positive people working together generates additional positivity. Even when the group dynamics become difficult, which is natural given the stress of fighting for survival, being part of a group is preferable to facing survival on your own. Remember, a lone wolf is still alone.

The cowboy mentality has no place in survival. Swallow your pride, ask for help, and focus on getting your group to gel. When you commit to survival, you are committing to providing yourself with the best resources possible to make it through. This includes getting people who care about you behind you and with you.

The Power of Visualization

Visualization might sound trendy, but it's long been respected by psychologists and clergy alike both for its simplicity and its effectiveness. You envision the future you want—in detail—then break down that image into its elements, make a plan, strategize set goals, make deadlines, build your model, and go for it.[22] I am constantly impressed by the power of visualization in my daily life and in *all* the successful people I've observed.

Recently I was watching the program *The 5 Keys to Mastery,* which featured an attention-grabbing anecdote about world-famous, Grammy Award-winning musician Carlos Santana. On his last day of high school, Santana told his friends that he was going to play with Eric Clapton. They laughed at him.

It almost didn't matter to Santana that his dream seemed so ludicrous. In his mind he was already playing with Clapton. He was on stage with him, rocking out, and living his dream. The crazy part is that, within a year of having that conversation, it came true!

I introduced you earlier in this chapter to Lee Ellis, whose memoir *Leading with Honor* is a wonderful and worthy read. (Lee graciously contributed his wisdom and perspectives for this book as well.) He fully understands the power of visualization. During his months at the Hanoi Hilton, he often retreated into his own mind. He spent months imagining his own forty-acre

---

22 "The Five Keys to Mastery," http://www.the5keystomastery.com/_ The%2B5%2BKeys.html.

farm. How could he best run it? What would he plant? How would he make the most money from the land? With plans for his farm in place, Lee decided he would become an attorney. He used the communication network among his fellow prisoners to ask advice about law schools and different kinds of law. He decided he would go to the University of Virginia and become a tax attorney. Some days he "played golf" by re-walking every course he'd ever been on. Other days he practiced typing on an imaginary machine.

Not surprisingly, Lee found real benefits to having used his time this way once he was released and returned to the States. He was faster at typing than he had been previously. His mental math was much better thanks to his calculations for his farm. And those forty acres he dreamed of? Five years after returning home, he purchased a sixty-four-acre farm outside of San Antonio. ("Hey, you got twenty-four extra acres!" I teased him.)

This is the power of *visualization*. By staying alert to the possibilities in the world and choosing to focus positively on your dreams, you see real change in your life. A prison cell in Hanoi couldn't contain Lee's mind. The adventures and experiences he built for himself gave him hope, but they also gave him ambition and focus once he was freed. If he hadn't spent time in prison figuring out what he wanted his life to look like, it might have been disorienting to return to the United States with a wealth of trauma and a dearth of plans.

This ability to have perspective while keeping hope is fundamental to survival. To echo Admiral Stockdale, you have to be realistic about your circumstances while maintaining your faith in your survival and yourself. Lee stayed grounded in the moment by being a part of the POW community and finding every possible method to resist his captors. He kept his faith in himself and his future alive by planning for the life he wanted.

Dreaming about a Better Life

I believe that every single one of us can benefit from the power of visualization. And I'd like to close this chapter by sharing a story about a woman who has always dreamed big despite the troughs of her chronically tumultuous life.

This last year, I took an Uber to the airport and started chatting with the driver, a wonderful lady named Verna Cooper. Verna immediately captivated me with her charisma and enthusiasm. She radiates positivity.

As we started talking, she began to share small pieces of her life story. I was so drawn in by her survival journey that I asked if I might interview her for this book. Honestly, it's difficult to capture in writing the impact Verna's experiences had on me. She is a force of nature in herself, and I can't seem to do her justice on the page, though I'll do my best.

Verna spent her high school years raising her younger siblings, only to become pregnant in her senior year. The baby's father was shipped off to Vietnam, but she busied herself working, saving money, and purchasing a house for them.

The house she bought was something she'd dreamed about endlessly. She had pictured it in her mind so clearly, down to the finest detail. The house was simple, painted blue and white like a bright sunny sky dotted with fluffy clouds. Its white picket fence accented the colors of the flowers that overflowed the clay pots on the spacious porch—where she alternately sat in a swing or a rocking chair. The house became a happy home with her in it. As Verna talked, even I was beginning to envision it. Her home had become a reality born from a vivid dream laced with action and attitude. She was all of twenty years old.

Verna, the dreamer and the doer

When her husband returned from the war, the marriage quickly ended. Verna lost everything, including the house. But she kept on. She had no choice. Too many people were depending on her—the theme of her life.

The young mother remarried, but her second husband fell into drugs. A third was unfaithful and ran off with her money. One of her children lit himself on fire by exploding a cap gun into a gas canister. A few years later this same child accidentally shot himself in the leg with an abandoned shotgun. Verna hauled him to the hospital just in time to save his life. All the while she battled her own health problems and the creep of bankruptcy. But she always knew what she wanted: a quiet, safe home—surrounded by a white picket fence—that would serve as a refuge for her family and herself.

Verna's troubles went from bad to heartbreaking. She lost a grandchild in a freak accident. Her mother passed away while Verna was undergoing a medical procedure, and Verna felt that she was to blame because of the stress she'd caused. Throughout it all she kept clinging fiercely to her dream of being back in her own home where she belonged.

Years later, as Verna was setting herself up in a new apartment, she got a call from the property manager of her original house. He asked if she'd be interested in coming back and renting it. "Can I make that happen?" Verna thought. She decided, *yes*, she could.

Within a month she was back in her very first home, and life finally felt manageable. Her home is and has always been her oasis, a gathering place for all her kids and grandkids where she finds her happiness. "Amidst all the tragedy and debt, I make it tranquil," she says.

Verna is always planning, always dreaming. Her positive mindset is how she has survived the ups and downs of her life. "It's not what you do, it's how you carry yourself when you do it."

Her happiness is infectious. Toward the end of the interview she laughingly explained that her biggest problem right now is that she looks so youthful, men much too young for her are always trying to ask her out!

This could have just been just another Uber ride, but for me it was a delightful discovery. Verna is someone who embodies the idea of positive visualization: envision a map to your dreams, and you will see them become a reality.

Survival journeys test the core of every person. Pain and loss are inevitable, but determine not to lose your ability to find small moments of happiness in the midst of them. Becoming bitter, resentful, full of self-pity, or self-centered is draining. You need every ounce of energy you have to survive.

Positive thinking actually gives you *more* energy (it's been proven, remember, that having a positive outlook adds years to your life). You need that extra energy if you want to continue the fight. Salvador Alvarenga got a boost whenever he saw a container ship sail by his small dinghy. The irony is that he knew they probably weren't going to rescue him, but they represented the chance that someday a ship might sail close enough for him to get someone's attention. That was enough.

It might be the magnificence of your surroundings that inspire you. Vast glaciers, tall mountains, and big seas can create big problems for people, but survivors trapped in avalanches or stranded in the ocean can see how majestic their surroundings are, how they are part of something bigger.

When it comes to survival, view happiness as though it's a set of monkey bars; visualize yourself swinging from one bar to the next and trying to hang on until you get to the end of your struggle.

Happiness in survival doesn't feel like real happiness because it's relative to how you felt in the happier times you've had. How can you be happy when facing terminal illness or a life-changing injury? Wade Hoag says that people ask him how he could possibly be happy again when he's no longer able to do also many of the things he loved. For him, it boils down to adaptation. "I have little hope I will walk again, just like Stefani Schaefer has little hope her husband will get better. But for me, and for her and her children, there is the promise of a better tomorrow."

So look beyond the superficial definition of happiness to what it means to be truly positive and grateful for the life you have. For me, I strongly believe that fighting for others is how you find your joy whether "others" are your family, friends, favorite charity, or all of the above.

Regardless of who you are, someone out there needs your help. It is counterintuitive, but reaching out to others is effective personal therapy. So many of the survivors I interviewed had taken note of others who were suffering more than them or were less fortunate. This put their own struggles in perspective.

CHAPTER 6

REACH IN ACTION:
WADE HOAG'S STORY

As I hope you've seen in the previous five chapters, the beauty of REACH is that it's not a complicated formula. When you are fighting for your survival, complex thinking goes out the window. REACH is five, easy intuitive steps: take responsibility for yourself and others; make an evaluation and a plan for how you'll survive; take action to implement that plan; maintain your confidence throughout those steps; and stay positive, finding happiness against the odds. Put together as a checklist to be followed in order, REACH is your best chance for survival.

REACH is also adaptable to your circumstances and beliefs. *Every survivor* in this book lived REACH in some form from start to finish. I chose to associate certain stories with specific elements but again, *every story contains every element.* Most of the folks you met used the REACH protocol not once but many times as they processed their initial trauma, survived survival, and then moved on to the rest of their life.

In the beginning of this book I told you that you would hear from my friend Wade Hoag. While I've been careful to focus on individual elements of REACH in the other stories in this book, I believe Wade's story is the perfect one to tie all five elements of REACH together.

In the late spring of 2015, Wade was living in Lake Tahoe working in construction, having just graduated from a demanding boy's preparatory school. One day at a job site he was standing on a lift three stories up with two other men to help set a window in place. Suddenly the lift tilted and the window the men were holding started to fall. In a split second, they could all be crushed under its weight. Wade acted instinctively and shoved one of the men out of the way of the toppling window. The other man on the lift did the same for Wade, pushing him off the lift and probably saving his life. Unfortunately, that shove would come at a cost.

Wade remembers lying on the ground, grateful to be alive, then realizing that he couldn't feel the lower half of his body. "I thought I'd been cut in half," he said. Feeling to his legs returned, along with tremendous pain. He figured his legs had been broken, and that was when he reached under his back and felt a coffee-cup-sized lump in his spine. He passed out.

When he woke up, he was in a hospital bed. He had survived the immediate danger . . . but was left with zero function from the waist down. For most teenage boys, this might be the end of their story. How do you go from life as an active, thrill-seeking adrenaline junkie—rock climbing, wrestling, skiing—to not being able to use your legs? Wade says he spent about a week going down this rabbit hole: What would have happened if he hadn't gone to Tahoe? What if he hadn't been at work that day? What if he'd fallen just a little differently?

Eventually, he realized he was going to drive himself crazy asking such unanswerable questions.

What happened next was both complete acceptance and utter denial of his new life. (Wade was beginning to apply to his own situation the Stockdale Paradox you read about in chapter 5.) "Yes, I am in a wheelchair. That's something I can't change right now. But I don't have to accept it." This step was his version of taking *responsibility*. The accident wasn't his fault. He couldn't control all the "what if's?" Instead of becoming wrapped up in his own struggle, Wade resolved to live as he had always wanted to—only now, however, it would be from his wheelchair. His mindset was the one thing he could control. Wade says it helps him to think that he isn't really unique in having to go through life with a limitation. "Everyone has their own sort of wheelchair."

I had met Wade years before his accident because his father and I are good friends. One beautiful summer afternoon at our community pool, he and I laughingly watched as teenage Wade was chatted up by every teenage girl at the pool. In the years that followed, Wade would head off on many adventures—Alaska, Tahoe, and who knows what else—and I could tell his dad lived vicariously through his daring, charismatic son. Seeing that same young man brought home to an entirely new life was shattering for Wade, his family, and his friends.

Adjusting to his new reality has been a process for Wade. Every night he dreams he's running. Upon waking, each day begins with this ritual: he cycles through the stages of grief, and then he listens to Warren Zevon's "My Shit's Fucked Up." It makes him laugh. After that, he's ready to meet the world. Half his battle is people's perception of him as a disabled person. "People try to push the wheelchair for me a lot," Wade shares. "The problem is people meet my disability before they meet me."

He is taking his new life one revolution at a time. Worrying about what will happen in the future—being able to dance at his wedding or to run around a yard chasing his own children—takes him down the rabbit hole again. Instead, he has to take his focus from the big picture down to the incremental. How am I going to get through today? What is my next physical challenge? *Evaluation* has to come to mean not just, "What is my long-term plan for dealing with my new life?" but "What are my plans for using the restroom today?" For him, coping is a daily struggle. As he says, he has been sentenced to life; there were times when dying felt easier.

Getting out of hospitals and clinics and into the world has been key in surviving survival for Wade. Choosing to make this a priority was his first moment of taking *action* rather than becoming a passive victim of the tragedy that befell him. Being able to connect with other people about his experience has also given him meaning. Wade recently spoke at his old high school about resilience and how to handle the unexpected curveballs life throws at you. Listening to him share such wisdom with his peers when he would be totally justified in feeling sorry for himself is incredibly inspiring.

That being said, I don't worry about Wade Hoag moving forward. Although mobility has been taken from him, his passion remains unbroken. As he says, he already knows how to survive tough stuff. His accident—and adjusting to life afterward—has given him a unique *confidence* and a renewed commitment to make his life better. Give him something else and he knows he can take it, just like watching a movie play out.

He is still deciding what to do with his future (remember, survival is incremental), but has already embarked on new adventures. Wade attends Hope College, which recently presented him its 2015-2016 Karen Page Courage award for contributions to the campus. Wade has been accepted into a trial for the Indego exoskeleton, a groundbreaking new structure that allows people with spinal cord injuries to walk again.

Wade has also decided that he wants to wheel across America. "My favorite scene in *Forrest Gump* was always him running across America," he says. He is already planning his journey for the summer of 2017, recruiting people for his camper crew and outfitting his specialty wheelchair. Apparently this feat has been accomplished before, so Wade has decided to set a new record time!

He has even started several businesses in his first year at Hope, including a venture capital fund. I've had the pleasure of acting as an investor (how can I possibly resist a deal with Wade?). "I can't climb mountains and trees anymore, so I start businesses instead," he explained to me. I sense that his deep passion and desire to make a significant difference in the world will take him to incredible heights. It will be fun to observe and continue in the honorable role of one of his Survival Cabinet members.

It's not all roses and sunshine. Sometimes we talk and he's ready to wheel across America. Other times the light at the end of the tunnel isn't as clear. For me, having a protocol as straightforward as REACH is comforting, but for Wade, at least right now, I don't think anything about survival feels clear-cut.

Rather than come at REACH directly, when Wade and I talk it tends to be in stories and metaphors. "Your life is a picture you're painting," I tell him. "When your accident happened, the whole thing got changed . . . but the paint hasn't dried. You're continuing to work on that painting every day with every choice you make and every action you take." The idea that survival is an ongoing process, but one that he can evolve and control, seems to give him some comfort. *Take some responsibility, make a plan, and keep acting* is what I'm really telling him. He just needs to hear it a different way—or lots of different ways.

Sometimes we discuss the stories of the survivors in this book. The most powerful message that encourages Wade is that we are not alone. Equally powerful is the message that other people have figured out how to get through it. Strikingly, Wade's own grandfather suffered a similar injury when he was 19 while storming the beach at Normandy on D-Day. He stepped on a grenade and was paralyzed, spending most of his life in a wheelchair. He then went on to become a highly successful entrepreneur and businessman. "People tell me I look and act exactly like him," Wade says, "He did all of these incredible things, and almost the exact same thing that happened to him happened to me."

If I told Wade to be *happy* about what has happened to him, he'd have every right to call me an insensitive asshole. Instead, we talk about Viktor Frankl and the magic of creating meaning by knowing you at least have control of your reactions to adversity. As Frankl teaches, you must rebel at the limits placed on you. You must maintain your sense of self and empathy toward others. You must always have something to fight for. And, no matter how ugly it gets, you must celebrate every sunrise. You have made it through one more night. This is now core to Wade's philosophy.

Explained in that way, Wade connects to the message that finding *happiness* is key to survival. (And so can you.) For example, surviving the fall but becoming paralyzed has made Wade more appreciative of what life has to offer. More "sensitive to life's rich flavors," is how he puts it. I think this is his version of *happy*. I can relate. If you've kept going beyond your darkest hour, at some point you notice that life becomes tolerable. When good things happen, you are really extra appreciative of them.

Wade has taken that thought and made it his own. Long after I had interviewed him for this book, he sent me an email to share an epiphany he'd had. His words were so eloquent and profound I instantly decided to include them in *Spinning into Control*.

> *We are all under the impression that identity and purpose are out there, somewhere, waiting to be discovered. We set off as young people searching for who we are only to realize that our purpose is inside us all along, waiting to be forged. Our identity lingers just beneath the skin, waiting to be set free.*
>
> *It is the most horrific parts of life that we forge into triumphs and meaning; it is through our trials that we build our identity. We cannot bear meaningless torment, but we can endure great pain if we believe there is meaning to be discovered. That doesn't mean you have to enjoy it. As I know, you can forge purpose and build identity but still be mad as hell.*
>
> *Your new "survivor" identity expands your vision of what it means to be human, while acknowledging that you cannot change what has happened to you. For me it is about shifting the narrative from "I am here, but I'm in a wheelchair" to "I am in a wheelchair, and I am here." That slight shift is significant. Now I am the one writing the story.*
>
> *Own the trials of your life. What looks like sorrow could be the gateway to a better existence filled with joy*

and triumph you never could have imagined. Remember,
the only story that matters is the one you're writing.

I am grateful that Wade became a part of my writing this book. He reminded me that survival doesn't feel clear when you're in the middle of it. He reminded me that at its most fundamental, survival becomes about getting up every day and making the choice to go on. He reminded me that survival is emotional and messy. That there's a place for protocols, but an even more important place for human connection. Wade has inadvertently used REACH to survive, but he couldn't have done it without his family, his friends, and the wide community of people who care about him. And he couldn't have done it without something to keep fighting for.

Your own survival journey will probably feel the same way. Messy, painful, unendurable. REACH is a tool you can make use of to organize the chaos as best you can, but you need to supply the motivation. How you choose to inject meaning into your survival story is up to you. For some people, it's religion. For me, it was my sons and Gina. For Wade, it's because he's simply not done adventuring.

CHAPTER 7

WRITING YOUR
NEXT CHAPTER

Survival situations can be over in moments or require years of endurance. You might find yourself flying through the REACH protocol in the space of several minutes, or you could be repeating the protocol again and again as your situation evolves, just like our survivors in this book have demonstrated. Either way, at some point your survival journey will reach the end of your particular battle.

For most of us, we start out expecting life to go well . . . until some kind of hardship hits us. Going through survival breaks the illusion that we are always safe, that everything will always end up okay. This is a painful loss, but it isn't a total loss. We gain something too.

We make it through our survival experience stronger than we were before. I know from personal experience that survival enhances your ability to appreciate and experience life. Your capacity for appreciation went from a max of 100 percent to

110 percent. You're more thankful for life's lulls because you know there are other adversities to overcome. You have become, through trials and suffering, a realistic optimist.

When another struggle inevitably comes your way, you are equipped with a fuller toolbox. Rather than going from 100 percent to 80 percent, however, you now go from 110 percent to 95 percent. Survival once again drives and deepens your ability to feel grateful for being alive, and you spike back up again—pushing past 110% to a new level. The graph that follows vividly shows how surviving terrible situations actually *increases* how much you appreciate your life and how getting to the other side of survival actually *raises* your baseline "happiness." In that spirit, when you experience a new setback, you don't fall as far into despair as you might have before because your capacity for positivity and resilience have been increased. Every struggle makes you stronger, boosting your confidence in yourself and your gratitude for your life. If you choose to let them, difficult experiences further define you and your character.

But, even with your enhanced appreciation for life, you will experience some days when the struggle doesn't feel as if it's over. For some people, the second part of the survival journey is harder than the first. Living with your survival experience can affect your life in profound ways. As Laurence Gonzales writes, you are no longer just living your life; you are—as his book title asserts—"surviving survival" (*Surviving Survival: The Art and Science of Resilience*).

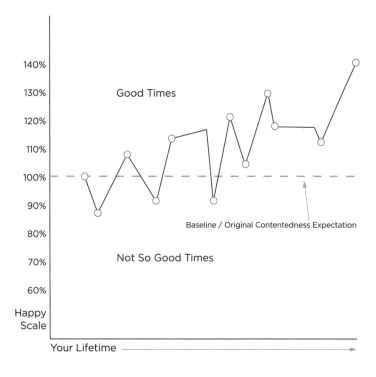

Just as everyone's survival journey looks different, your ability to move past and integrate your survival experience into your life will differ too. There can be positive outcomes from having undergone a survival experience: a new perspective, increased gratitude, and practiced resilience. There can be negative carryovers as well, both physical and psychological. Until you are on the other side of the journey, it's difficult to know what your own residual effects will be.

My goal with this chapter isn't to impart yet another protocol or viewpoint. Like I said, the way people internalize survival varies dramatically. Instead, I want to explore how some of the survivors already mentioned in this book adapted to life after survival. Some people truly experienced darkness in the aftermath of their moment of crisis. I will share their stories, including how they eventually were able to start reconstructing their lives and including their insistence on finding strength in the painful parts of their survival. Then we will discuss three strategies you can use to help you adjust to your new life: sharing your experience, finding community, and giving back.

The message of this chapter is that the story isn't over after surviving a traumatic, life-changing event. Now you need to write your epilogue, to survive your survival.

The Dark Side of Survival

In the research I did for this book, something that was emphasized again and again in survival epilogues was the idea that you will live with your survival experience for the rest of your life. It's the Alcoholics Anonymous philosophy of "I *am* an alcoholic" rather than "I *was* an alcoholic." You *are* a survivor rather than you *survived* something bad that happened to you.

Laurence Gonzales says it best using the metaphor of stranded mountaineers: "In some ways, we are always on the mountain." I have found this to be true of every survivor I interviewed. Stefani Schaefer (who you met in chapter 1) summed it up neatly: "We will never stop 'surviving.'" In other words, her life has been profoundly and permanently changed. Living through a scenario where your life or way of living is on the line inevitably alters you. In ways both positive and negative, you will always carry this experience with you.

For some people, their post-survival lives can be a struggle, even more so than was their initial survival scenario. They have a difficult time processing what happened or adjusting to the ways their life has changed. This can manifest as an "innocence lost"; they end up jaded and bitter about what they have been put through. Perhaps they even carry guilt about why they survived while others didn't make it. Chris Mintz, lauded as a hero by so many people, wrote on his Facebook page on Thanksgiving that all he could think of was the people who wouldn't be able to share the occasion with their families. At the same time, he's tremendously grateful for the outpouring of support—even a Kickstarter page for his medical bills—that people have shown him.

Still other survivors become extremely risk adverse: for example, they refuse to get on airplanes or to swim in the ocean—anything that feels like it increases the chances of being put in another survival scenario, rational or not. Their paranoia affects their ability to lead a normal life. The opposite is also true, although less common. Survivors grappling with a return to everyday life can obsessively seek out high-risk, adrenaline-laden challenges.

The extreme form of carrying your survival experience with you is posttraumatic stress disorder, or PTSD. This is a serious anxiety disorder wherein the person affected can have flashbacks that make them feel as if they are literally still living the trauma they experienced. War veterans are commonly at risk for PTSD, given the assault-based trauma they experience firsthand. While it is classified as a disorder, I want to stress that PTSD is a completely normal reaction to having been exposed to trauma. Many sufferers of PTSD berate themselves for not being able to "kick it," but it's not a function of being tough or weak. Trauma changes your brain physiology in a way that even the most resilient survivors cannot control. Part of the journey with PTSD is forgiving yourself for having it.

The fact is that combat veterans are still people, subject to the same emotions as the rest of us. Just because their survival

epilogues do not wrap up neatly doesn't diminish the importance of their stories. If anything, it is just as important to share
"part two" of the survival story. You can draw inspiration from
the idea that surviving is hard, but coming home is equally hard.
You are not weak because you have made it to the other side of
your survival scenario and are still struggling.

This struggle is yet another step in survival. Remember,
some of us are always "on the mountain." The event never stops
happening to you because you are fundamentally changed. People who have been confined to wheelchairs are always reminded
of their new reality (ask Wade Hoag). People who have lost
loved ones in car crashes are always reminded of their loss when
they get into a car. Even if the accident is over, the wounds can
be reopened. Survival is never neatly wrapped up. It doesn't end
when the test results come back negative, when a helicopter
spots your life raft, or when you finish reading this book.

Further on in this chapter you'll read about how you can
take back control and integrate your survival experience into
your new life. I want to highlight, however, that PTSD is a
serious condition. If you find yourself experiencing any of the
symptoms of PTSD, I strongly recommend that you seek help.
It is normal to be impacted by traumatic events, especially ones
in which your life as you know it has been threatened. You are
not the first to walk this path; multiple survivors featured in this
book suffered severe PTSD after returning home. Tugboat cook
Harrison Okene (chapter 4) and fisherman Salvador Alvarenga
(chapter 5) both had difficulty being near water or boats after
their experiences on the high seas. Many of the thirty-three men
who had been trapped in the San Jose, Chile, mine (chapter 3)
experienced terrible nightmares, could not be in enclosed rooms,
or had difficulty interacting with their friends and family after

they were freed. Some went the opposite route and returned to the mines.

I was poignantly made aware of PTSD when I met Marcus Luttrell, former US Navy SEAL and author of *Lone Survivor*, shortly after he was discharged due to injury and had begun a speaking tour. My YPO chapter was one of his first stops. Marcus had a friend with him to help manage the event. As I walked through the auditorium door, the friend, who was holding a basket full of cell phones, stopped me. He explained that Marcus was still dealing with the trauma of his time in Iraq. If someone forgot to silence their phone and it abruptly went off, Marcus was liable to go ballistic. So, if I wouldn't mind handing over my . . . I pretty much threw my phone into the basket, so eager was I not to see a Navy SEAL take down a room of executives.

I share this encounter because although we expect our warriors to come home from battle with physical scars, we are not always aware of the psychological ones. Marcus Luttrell is physically one of the toughest dudes ever yet even he wasn't immune to PTSD. As I shook his hand after the presentation, it was clear he was still struggling. You could see it in his eyes.

I also urge you to read the story of Cheyeanne Fitzgerald, one of the Oregon shooting victims.[23] Cheyeanne survived being shot by the same gunman that Chris Mintz tried to disarm, and her life has been fundamentally altered. Not only does she carry the physical scars of the attack, her PTSD and the resulting isolation has been extreme, profoundly affecting her as well as her family. A profile of her journey in the *Washington*

---

23 Eli Saslow, "A Survivor's Life," *The Washington Post*, December 5, 2015. http://www.washingtonpost.com/sf/national/2015/12/05/after-a-mass-shooting-a-survivors-life/.

Post is one of the most raw and moving examples of PTSD that I have encountered.

The examples are endless. You are not alone. Fortunately, there are resources out there to help you find healthy ways to heal.

Finding Courage in Vulnerability

Trauma haunts more than just veterans. Victims of assault and abuse also experience high rates of posttraumatic stress but with additional layers of shame and guilt. As I was completing this book, the 2016 Stanford rape case was making headlines. Brock Turner, a freshman at the university, was caught sexually assaulting an unconscious young woman behind a dumpster at a frat party.

Despite having been hauled off her body and attempting to flee the scene of the crime, Turner and his lawyers decided to take the case to court, arguing that the young woman had consented to his advances before passing out. Neither his victim nor the jury agreed with his version of events. Turner was unanimously convicted on three counts: assault with intent to commit rape of an intoxicated woman, sexually penetrating an intoxicated person with a foreign object, and sexually penetrating an unconscious person with a foreign object.

This caught national headlines for two reasons: First, the judge handed down a sentence far more lenient than the minimum recommendation, sparking outrage. Second (and this is what I want to keep the focus on), the 7,244-word statement the victim read at Turner's sentencing is both heartbreaking and beautiful. This young woman endured a violation that is unimaginable and then had to continually revisit her trauma during the long trial. She was blamed and shamed for her actions—getting drunk—while excuses were made for her rapist's behavior.

Her statement details the fragments she remembers of the night she was assaulted, including being extensively and intimately photographed by hospital nurses before being allowed to walk home in clothes loaned to her (hers were kept by the police for evidence) and her emotions as she underwent the trial. She was told that she should be prepared to lose. Because she was unconscious when the assault happened, she couldn't technically prove she hadn't said yes.

I am especially struck by the phrase in which she thanks her therapist for helping her "find courage in vulnerability." Finding this courage enabled her to find her *why*—that fundamental question you must ask when you face your nightmares. Her statement ends on this powerful note.

> *And finally, to girls everywhere, I am with you. On the nights when you feel alone, I am with you. When people doubt you or dismiss you, I am with you. I fought every day for you. So never stop fighting, I believe you. As the author Anne Lamott once wrote, "Lighthouses don't go running all over an island looking for boats to save; they just stand there shining."*
>
> *Although I can't save every boat, I hope that by speaking today, you absorbed a small amount of light . . . and a big, big knowing that you are important, unquestionably, you are untouchable, you are beautiful, you are to be valued, respected, undeniably, every minute of every day, you are powerful and nobody can take that away from you.*

It is clear that this horrific and prolonged experience will be part of her life forever, but she is training her mind to persevere by helping others, thereby making her message indelible in her mind as well. Her survival journey, instead of breaking her, has made her stronger.

Coming Back Stronger

Integrating your survival experience into your life in a positive way can take many forms, but most of the survivors I researched and talked to shared these similar strategies for their life post-survival: share your experience; find community; give back; and embrace your new life—all while remembering to forgive yourself.

Share Your Experience

One of the best ways people recovered from their survival experience was by sharing their experience. As you can see just by reading this book, many of the extreme survivors wrote books, gave interviews, or became motivational speakers. By writing or talking about their experiences, the survivors took time to examine their survival journeys. Their experience became not a trauma that had happened to them but a narrative of how they were faced with something crummy and ended up the hero of their own story.

This is their way of seeking the "new normal." It's natural to look back and wish your life could be like it was before the trauma. You can find freedom in connecting the pieces of what happened to change your life and add meaning to how that change has proven your resilience.

Oftentimes survivors who take the time to do an in-depth analysis of their experience end up with striking insights about how to live because of their struggles. A wonderful example of this is Viktor Frankl's powerful book *Man's Search for Meaning*. Instead of losing himself to despair after witnessing the atrocities of Auschwitz, Dachau, and other concentration camps, Frankl created a philosophy that gave meaning to suffering and empowered victims. While we cannot choose our circumstances, he wrote, we can always choose how we react to and feel about what has happened to us. This, in effect, is freedom. He and his fellow prisoners carried a sense of pride for maintaining this freedom.

Part of the benefit of reading about and meeting survivors is that it helps put into perspective the problems we face. But I caution you against comparing your story to what others have been through. As my friend Steve McPeake says, there is no one-upsmanship when it comes to misery. Everyone has problems that feel—and are—significant.

No matter what you are facing, you can use the examples and tools of survivors to help guide you. Similarly, your story might be useful to someone else. After all, isolation can be a survivor's worst enemy.

Find Community

Sharing your experience also allows you to find community. Opening up the story of your survival experience then opens the door to people supporting you. Because Stefani Schaefer (you'll recall her from chapter 1) is a popular broadcast news anchor in Cleveland, she publicly shares updates about her husband Roger and her family's journey with her viewers. While she says it is disheartening to give annual updates about Roger because his medical condition has not improved, the outpouring of support from people she has never met has meant the world to her. She has boxes and boxes of letters that she has kept that she turns to when she needs a boost. (Stefani has also had chances to help others who are facing challenges, as you'll read about in the box titled "Give Back" further on in the chapter.)

By sharing your story you will meet people who have been through similar experiences. Stefani recounts how one day she was at her children's school when a mother she had never met approached her expressing condolences. The woman shared that her father had been diagnosed with Alzheimer's and she had been charged with taking care of him. Just like Roger, the woman's father no longer knew who the people around him were and needed help with even the most basic tasks. "The difference is, this is my father," the woman said. "I get to go home at night. I don't know how you're doing it."

It was like a lightbulb going off for Stefani. She hadn't realized how burned out she was until the woman, who was able to empathize with some of what she was going through, asked. That moment was a real turning point for her as she began to build a new life centered on the reality that her husband might never recover from his traumatic brain injury. All because of a chance conversation that had been sparked by Stefani's openness about her family's struggles.

Give Back

Almost every survivor who shares their experiences also seems to become motivated to give back to their community. I believe this is a key part of surviving survival. Nothing puts your own journey into perspective like helping others in need. (Which is exactly what the heartwarming story in the following box titled "Survival as a Team Effort," goes to show.)

Giving back takes different forms. Helping others with the

wisdom gained in your survival experiences, for example, can become your life mission. Frank Iszak, whom you met in chapter 3, wrote his life story because he wanted to illustrate the importance of safeguarding personal liberty (something he feels is slipping away, even in America). This is a topic that he speaks about passionately in regard to today's political climate.

Iszak also founded a yoga studio for the elderly, feeling similarly passionate about the need for older people to take care of their bodies and minds. Speaking with a man who had gone from hijacker refugee to yogi made me feel like just about anything was possible.

SURVIVAL AS A TEAM EFFORT

Survivors who are, for the most part, on the other side of their experiences remember that they are beholden to others. When people around them are struggling, they feel compelled to "pay it forward." Stefani Schaefer, who already does so much for the community, had a unique chance to do so this last year.

After Alex passed, Rick became deeply enmeshed in his struggle to figure out what his life would look like with Alex no longer in it. One day Rick stumbled upon a man selling Golden Retriever puppies. One in particular caught his eye and he couldn't resist picking it up.

"How old is this pup?" Rick asked.

"He was born May 14," the man answered. The day Alex died. And just like that Leo the new pup had found a permanent home.

Not surprisingly, Rick and Leo—with his practically karmic link to Rick's beloved son—were inseparable.

During the Christmas holidays, however, Rick left Leo outside one morning for just a moment while he stepped back inside to grab his morning coffee. As Rick turned back to fetch Leo, the puppy was nowhere to be found. Vanished. No trace.

This was strange. Leo never left the yard and always stayed as close to Rick as possible. Rick began to search desperately. Panic ensued at the thought of the many mishaps that could have befallen him: cars, coyotes, bone-chilling December cold, endless neighboring woods —the same ones where Alex lost his life.

Rick knew who to call: the well-known Cleveland expert in dog rescue of any kind, my very own wife, Gina. Her company, Dogs Unlimited Rescue, rescues hundreds of animals in need every year.

We were out of town on holiday vacation with Stefani Schaefer and her family, which could have made Gina's involvement tricky. Not so. All holiday festivities came to a screeching halt while she sounded the horn for the "troops" to mobilize. Her selfless and devoted posse was in action within minutes, a dragnet of large-scale proportions.

Stefani immediately called Fox 8, which quickly disseminated the word around town. "THE SEARCH FOR LEO" was the number one story for days; thousands in the community knew the link between Rick's grieving for Alex and Leo's healing companionship. Gina suggested raising the reward to record levels to tempt both rescuers and dognappers. It worked!

Stefani and Gina reading an early version of the manuscript.

A tipster, who turned out to be an accomplice to Leo's dognapper, decided to turn in his partner-in-crime before the perpetrator could collect the sum. It seems the guilty party was a former acquaintance of Alex's who saw in Rick and Leo's closeness the potential for ransom.

Based on the tip, Rick and his friend Wendy went to the alleged hiding place to claim Leo. When the perpetrator's mother answered the door, she denied the presence of a dog—even as a dog barked incessantly in the basement. As Rick ran for the back door, Leo came running to a window to greet his human soul mate.

I'm struck by the magic that happened when everyone came together to support Rick. Gina, Stefani, and the legions of volunteers who knew what Leo meant to Rick after Alex's passing cared enough to donate their time to finding the puppy. All of them took responsibility for Leo's disappearance, even when it wasn't their concern, contributed to recovering him, and celebrated his safe return.

My friend Steve McPeake, whose daughter Maurin is profoundly mentally and physically disabled, has devoted his entire life to serving people with such disabilities. He felt Maurin was not given the care or attention she deserved in the homes she was placed in. Instead of giving into resentment, Steve's life became about service. Since 1985 he has been the president and CEO of North Coast Community Homes, an organization that houses people with mental and developmental disabilities. His dedication and passion have changed the lives of thousands of people.

Since retiring, Lee Ellis has made his life's work consulting, writing, and speaking about authentic, honorable leadership. He believes that integrity starts with our leaders, whether they work in the military, government, or private sector. Lee lives out his beliefs in his professional and personal life. His "epilogue" is a wonderful example of how experiencing trauma can unearth your courage. Lee shared with me that, after returning from Vietnam, he felt much less inhibited by his fears than he had before his experience as a POW. He knew what it was like to face darkness head-on and dive in, coming out the other side a survivor. This gave him the confidence to face fears in his new life.

For example, after a stressful period, his wife asked if they might go to counseling to help work through some of their issues. You would think a warrior and revered veteran would hesitate to agree to visit a marriage counselor at a time when others in our culture might view it as a potential sign of personal weakness.

"No!" Lee says confidently. "I have faced real humiliation and true degradation of the human spirit enough that I don't worry what other people think of me. It's another call to get to work and support those I love and serve without hesitation or my personal feelings." The pair saw the counselor and their issues were swiftly and lovingly resolved.

Embrace Your New Life

When my helicopter safely landed back at the airport, I didn't know I had been handed a second chance at life. It was a miracle that the helicopter, with its cracked blade, had made it back to the hangar without disintegrating and falling out of the sky.

I could have refused to ever get into any aircraft—let alone a helicopter—again. But flying was my passion. I knew the risks. I resolved to be better prepared. Freed from my divorce battle and finally able to start rebuilding my business, it was time to start my new life. After all, I had what was important: my children, my parents, my health, and my fiancée, Gina.

The insurance company declared the helicopter totaled. I was still in the process of trying to dig out financially. A new helicopter was well out of my price range, but a totaled one wasn't. I bought that helicopter out of salvage and completely refurbished it, hiring the same mechanic who had seen the helicopter miraculously make it home.

Today I own the helicopter that almost took my life. I fly it regularly. Inherent in life is risk; it's just a matter of being well prepared when disaster strikes. My risk with the helicopter I spun onto an on-ramp years ago is mitigated. I know what was wrong with that helicopter, and I know I've fixed it. I was prepared when I started to spin out of control that dark day in 2010, and I'm even better prepared now. I have to be; my life after survival is worth fighting for.

When everything falls apart, our first instinct is to assume that life as we know it is over. Nothing will ever be the same. Every survivor I talked to (myself included) felt this way. Yet, sometimes we are treated to glimpses of our former life. I'd like to close this chapter with an example of a dream come true that I never expected in surviving survival.

When all the financial restraining orders were taken out against my businesses during my divorce, I really thought I was done on all levels. Rather than foreclose on my properties, I tried to find ways to keep them afloat. One property in particular, a beautiful beach house in Florida that we had bought to develop, was sold for pennies to a discount buyer.

The happy ending is that, once I was back on my feet again, I monitored the property. Sure enough, it went back up for sale, and I was able to buy it. My mom always dreamt of retiring to the serenity of the beach after a lifetime spent juggling children, running an ER, a working farm, and a traveling husband. My parents live in that house now. Once my Achilles heel, that beach house became a dream come true for my mom. Her gratitude means more to me than anything, especially after all the love and support she has given me.

Fighting for survival and emerging into a new reality gave my life new meaning. As it turns out, life on the other side of survival can be better than the life you had before, even if you have been changed by pain or loss. Admittedly, using the word "better" might be a stretch, but you will learn lessons about yourself and life that are worth having. There is light at the end of the tunnel, even if you have days (or months) (or years) when you can't see it.

Being a survivor gives you an extra responsibility to live the life you have wanted. You know what it feels like to potentially have everything taken away. It's okay if it takes you some time to get there; like Wade Hoag says, it's an incremental process. Surviving survival is about taking it one page at a time, until finally you are writing chapters that take you to the epilogue your survival journey deserves.

THE OPPOSITE
OF DEATH IS LOVE

Where my forties had been marked by divorce and financial distress and having to totally rebuild my life, I found myself writing new chapters as I approached my fiftieth birthday. I was genuinely looking forward to the next decade—something I could never have imagined just a few years earlier. I wanted to commemorate this journey with something to mark the achievement. I decided to climb Mount Kilimanjaro in Tanzania, the tallest freestanding mountain in the world and, at 19,341 feet, the highest peak in Africa.

Originally I was hoping one of my sons could accompany me, but neither could make it. I called my father to commiserate when, to my surprise, he eagerly volunteered to come. As soon as I invited him—really, he invited himself—I realized it might have been a bad idea. After all, this was a serious endeavor. What if he went and something terrible happened? Was it even realistic to think he could make it?

He immediately showed me he was serious about preparation. We both began exercising vigorously. In addition to time at the gym, he would put on a pack and go climb stadiums and local steep hillsides.

Our preparation went beyond exercise. Under the advice of my good friend Brian Coughlin, a self-educated and experienced expert on Kilimanjaro, we added other physical preparations to our regimens. We both slept in Hypoxico altitude chambers. My father went and had a custom portable sleep apnea (C-pap) machine made (his doctor told him he wouldn't make the summit without having the machine in tow, and we couldn't drag his normal machine all the way to the top). Everything we could do to prepare, we did. We had never attempted anything like this before, and both of us wanted this trip to be a successful one.

The hike up Kilimanjaro is not an easy one. The traditional route takes almost a week from the trailheads. You hike through jungle, emerge from the treeline, and find yourself up in a freezing, unearthly crater braving significant winds, sleet, and snow—not to mention nausea and breathless panting after a crushing climb.

We didn't do the climb alone. I had found a guiding organization that took groups of climbers up the mountain. Climbing with people you've never met is precarious; you're trusting them with your safety, after all. My father's approach, influenced by his years in human capital, was very interesting. He immediately went about getting to know the guides and other climbers. He knew that if we bonded, that would increase our chances of success due to team cohesion. He treated the guides, porters, and other climbers with the utmost respect.

The effect of his conscious teambuilding was that he became a rallying point for the group. Our mission wasn't just to climb for ourselves, but to get him to the top (he says the same about me). As it turned out, we probably shouldn't have worried. He believed 100 percent in his ability to make it, even when things went wrong. His C-pap machine quit several days in. I thought that was the end of the trip for him, but he told me not to worry. He was right. His physical stats—heart rate, for example—were better than those of the youngest climber, a twenty-year-old man.

At about 14,000 feet, two hours before the end of Day 3, we slowly approached an imposing cliff called the Barranco Wall. It had been a truly grueling day of trekking. Topping out at an 850-foot sheer wall of lava rock that halted all forward progress was haunting. We all scraped our way toward the featureless barrier, lungs burning and muscles aching. We would need all our energy to reach the top of the cliff the next day. It was still another two days to the summit.

That night we set up camp at the foot of the wall, a looming reminder of what we would face the next day. A cold wind whistled over us as I struggled to shove food into my upset stomach. As I lay in my sleeping bag that night, I stared into the blackness, trying to visualize the challenge ahead of us. I imagined what it would be like to pull myself and my backpack over boulders and slippery scree. I was scared for myself and for my father. We had trained diligently, but nothing about running in the comfort of the high school stadium was like the behemoth wall that squatted in front of us.

What had I gotten myself into? And what had I gotten my *father* into (I was reminded of his presence listening to his bear-like snores)? Sure, I had set myself up for failure, but had I set him up for injury? Or worse? I needed to plan, to come up with a strategy for getting us help in the event something happened!

My exhausted mind rejected sleep and desperately tried to form some incoherent rescue plan. I had spiraled down the hole into irrational, illogical, catastrophic thoughts. I was a mess.

What seemed like seconds later, a flashlight came tapping at my tent. I had somehow nodded off. Time to pack up and buck up. Nothing else to be done.

So, I got pissed. That was the only emotion I had left after my horrible night. As we approached the bottom of the wall, I could see small blue and red glowing dots scattered on the cliff face above. Headlamps, I realized. Those dots were the headlamps of people who had already started the climb and were struggling above us. I was soon to be a pissed-off dot among the many, trying desperately to keep on.

We started up. Step by step. No one spoke. I wasn't the only one feeling anxious. My father, however, was downright sunny. He flashed me a smile as if we were headed off for a day of fishing.

Slowly and deliberately or, as our guides constantly chanted in Swahili—*polé, polé*—we traversed, sidestepped, climbed, and stumbled. Halfway up the cliff there's a passage called the Kissing Wall. The trail gets so skinny that you have to press your face to the wall, firmly hold the rock, and sidestep in the hopes that you can offset the weight of your pack from pulling you into the four-hundred-foot drop behind you. (I think there's still an imprint of my face there.) I grabbed our guide's hand and leapt from rock to rock.

My total focus on my survival meant that I didn't notice when we topped out and struggled over the Barranco Wall. We had made it: above the wall, above the clouds. The insurmountable obstacle that had haunted my dreams the night before had been eliminated.

Temporary relief routed my obsession with pain and failure.

At least for a day, we had come out on top, taking the journey *polé, polé,* one step at a time.

The summit day was a nine-hour-and-forty-minute push to the top that started in the early-morning moonlit hours. I had barely slept the previous night, worrying about how my father was going to do. Again, he knew he was going to make it and what he had to do to get there.

As I sluggishly approached my father as we set foot on the summit, my oxygen-deprived mind could muster only these profane yet profoundly respectful words: "YOU are ONE TOUGH Son of a Bitch!" I gasped as I bear-hugged him and patted his snow-dusted back, then stared into his steel blue triumphant eyes.

Standing on top of that mountain almost twenty thousand feet above the African plains on Father's Day 2014 with my seventy-nine-year-old father was the ultimate triumph for me. Surviving how far I'd fallen in the years before, I was finally on top again. Sharing that moment with him meant the world to me. It was an emotional moment.

And then my next thought was: Let's get the hell back down this mountain!

As we quickly descended, I turned fifty years old. A birthday cake—arranged by Gina from thousands of miles away—waited for me at the lodge.

The summit was special in more ways than one. For one, my father became at the time the oldest American—at seventy-nine-and-three-quarters—to climb Kilimanjaro. We also raised fifty thousand dollars for people with disabilities. It made the difference for both of us that the climb would have a positive impact beyond ourselves.

Dad once said to me, "Life ain't about how fast you run or how high you climb, but how well you bounce." I think this is true. Getting through life isn't about achievement; it's about resilience. My survival journey proved that to me time and time again.

Getting back on my feet wasn't motivated by money or notoriety. I love building my business and being able to play a positive role in my community, but deciding to keep going when everything was burning down around me came down to the people I loved. My kids, Gina, my parents, my friends—that's why I knew I had to make it. Just like Nando Parrado says, the opposite of death isn't life; it's love. Summiting Kilimanjaro meant something to me, but not nearly as much as summiting Kilimanjaro *with my father* after surviving the pain and turmoil of the prior decade.

Chase, Pat, and Logan

If you find yourself amid the wreckage and are wondering how you can ever keep going, remembering the people who love and need you is the only thing you can do. I know it sounds trite, but every survivor in this book had something or someone they were surviving for. Putting yourself outside your suffering is how you find the strength to take the first REACH step and start the process of spinning yourself INTO control.

SURVIVOR'S LIBRARY

Introduction

Defoe, Daniel. *Robinson Crusoe*. Available at Project Gutenberg: http://www.gutenberg.org/files/521/521-h/521-h.htm

Ellis, Lee. *Leading with Honor: Leadership Lessons from the Hanoi Hilton*. FreedomStar Media, 2014.

Hillenbrand, Laura. *Unbroken: A World War II Story of Survival, Resilience, and Redemption*. New York: Random House Trade Paperback, 2014.

Luttrell, Marcus, and Patrick Robinson. *Lone Survivor: The Eyewitness Account of Operation Redwing and the Lost Heroes of SEAL Team 10*. Boston: Little, Brown and Co., 2013.

Weir, Andy. *The Martian*. New York: Broadway Books, 2014.

Chapter 1: Responsibility

Deleo, Peter. *Survive! My Fight for Life in the High Sierras*. Robson Books, 2005.

Frankl, Viktor E. *Man's Search for Meaning*. Boston, Beacon Press, 2006.

Gonzales, Laurence. *Deep Survival: Who Lives, Who Dies, and Why.* New York: W. W. Norton & Company, 2004.

Parrado, Nando. *Miracle in the Andes: 72 Days on the Mountain and My Long Trek Home.* New York: Broadway Books, 2007.

Chapter 2: Evaluation

Maclean, Norman. *Young Men and Fire.* Chicago: University of Chicago Press, 1992.

Ripley, Amanda. *The Unthinkable: Who Survives when Disaster Strikes—and Why.* New York: Harmony, 2009.

Viesturs, Ed, and David Roberts. *K2: Life and Death on the World's Most Dangerous Mountain.* New York: Crown Archetype, 2009.

Chapter 3: Action

DiJulius, John R., III. *The Customer Service Revolution: Overthrow Conventional Business, Inspire Employees, and Change the World.* Austin, TX: Greenleaf Book Group LLC, 2015.

Iszak, Frank. *Free for All to Freedom.* CreateSpace Independent Publishing Platform, 2011.

Tobar, Hector. *Deep Down Dark: The Untold Stories of 33 Men Buried in a Chilean Mine, and the Miracle That Set Them Free.* Picador, 2015.

Chapter 4: Confidence

Millard, Candice. *The River of Doubt: Theodore Roosevelt's Darkest Journey.* New York: Broadway Books, 2006.

Weathers, Beck, with Stephen G. Michaud. *Left for Dead: My Journey Home from Everest.* Villard, 2000.

Chapter 5: Happiness

Collins, Jim. *Good to Great: Why Some Companies Make the Leap and Others Don't.* Harper Business, 2001.

Covey, Stephen R. *The 7 Habits of Highly Effective People.* New York: Simon & Schuster, 2013.

Dweck, Carol S. *Mindset: The New Psychology of Success.* New York: Ballantine Books, 2007.

Gupta, Sanjay, M.D. *Chasing Life: New Discoveries in the Search for Immortality to Help You Age Less Today.* Wellness Central, 2008.

Duckworth, Angela. *Grit: The Power of Passion and Perseverance.* New York: Scribner, 2016.

Herfkens, Annette. *Turbulence: A True Story of Survival.* Matter & Mind, 2014.

Chapter 7: Writing Your Next Chapter

Gonzales, Laurence. *Surviving Survival: The Art and Science of Resilience.* New York: W.W. Norton & Company, 2013.

Kyle, Chris, and Scott McEwen. *American Sniper: The Autobiography of the Most Lethal Sniper in U.S. Military History.* HarperCollins, 2013.

Additional Resources

Memoirs

Beah, Ishmael. *A Long Way Gone: Memoirs of a Boy Soldier.* Sarah Crichton Books, 2008. (Sierra Leone Child Soldier)

Frank, Anne. *The Diary of a Young Girl.* Bantam, 1993. (Holocaust)

Ilibagiza, Immaculée. *Left to Tell: Discovering God Amidst the Rwandan Holocaust.* Hay House, Inc., 2014. (Rwandan Genocide)

Krakauer, Jon. *Into Thin Air: A Personal Account of the Mt. Everest Disaster.* Anchor, 1999. (Mountaineering)

Simpson, Joe. *Touching the Void: The True Story of One Man's Miraculous Survival*. Perennial, 2004. (Mountaineering)

Wiesel, Elie, and Marion Wiesel. *Night*. Hill and Wang, 2006. (Holocaust)

Non-fiction Survival Accounts

Des Pres, Terrence. *The Survivor: Anatomy of Life in the Death Camps*. Oxford University Press, 1980. (Nazi and Soviet Death Camps)

Griffith, Cary J. *Lost in the Wild: Danger and Survival in the Northwoods*. Borealis Books, 2007. (Wilderness Survival)

Junger, Sebastian. *The Perfect Storm: A True Story of Men Against the Sea*. New York: W. W. Norton & Company, 2009.

Kearns, David A. *Where Hell Freezes Over: A Story of Amazing Bravery and Survival*. Thomas Dunne Books, 2005. (Antarctic Plane Crash)

Lansing, Alfred, and Nathaniel Philbrick. *Endurance: Shackleton's Incredible Voyage*. New York: Basic Books, 2015. (Antarctic Survival)

Philbrick, Nathaniel. *In the Heart of the Sea: The Tragedy of the Whaleship* Essex. New York: Penguin Books, 2001.

Ralston, Aron. *Between a Rock and a Hard Place*. Atria, 2004. (Wilderness Survival)

Read, Piers Paul. *Alive: The Story of the Andes Survivors*. Avon, 2002. (Andes Plan Crash)

Roberts, David. *Alone on the Ice: The Greatest Survival Story in the History of Exploration*. New York: W. W. Norton & Company, 2014. (Antarctic Survival)

Stanton, Doug. *In Harm's Way: The Sinking of the USS* Indianapolis *and the Extraordinary Story of Its Survivors*. Owl Books, 2003.

Zuckerman, Peter, and Amanda Padoan. *Buried in the Sky: The Extraordinary Story of the Sherpa Climbers on K2's Deadliest Day*. New York. W. W. Norton & Company, 2013. (Mountaineering)

Zuckoff, Mitchell. *Frozen in Time: An Epic Story of Survival and a Modern Quest for Lost Heroes of World War II*. Harper Perennial, 2014. (Greenland Plane Crash)

Self-Help

Andrews, Andy. *The Traveler's Gift: Seven Decisions that Determine Personal Success.* Thomas Nelson, 2005. (Parable)

Brown, Brené. *Rising Strong: The Reckoning. The Rumble. The Revolution.* Spiegel & Grau, 2015.

Greitens, Eric. *Resilience: Hard-Won Wisdom for Living a Better Life.* Mariner Books, 2016. (Navy SEAL)

Moore, Christian. *The Resilience Breakthrough: 27 Tools for Turning Adversity into Action.* Greenleaf Book Group Press, 2014.

Moorhead, Jim. *The Instant Survivor: Right Ways to Respond when Things Go Wrong.* Austin, TX: Greenleaf Book Group Press, 2012.

Sherwood, Ben. *Survivor's Club: The Secrets and Science that Could Save Your Life.* Grand Central Publishing, 2010.

Siebert, Al. *The Survivor Personality: Why Some People Are Stronger, Smarter, and More Skillful at Handling Life's Difficulties . . . and How You Can Be Too.* TarcherPerigee, 2010.

SPECIAL APPRECIATION
AND ACKNOWLEDGMENTS

To my sons Logan and Chase, now well into your young adult lives.

You were thirteen and fifteen years old when your world shifted from under you as in an earthquake: The sudden end of all you had known and understood. The death of a family.

You would no longer sit around the same table for dinner. No longer the same safe place to sleep or the routines so cherished. Cast out into the swirl of the unknown unable to stop the spinning in a world where divorce is so commonplace that little attention was paid by others. A father's guilt and sense of failure. I take responsibility for finding no other way to avoid the mayhem, as hard as I tried. The forces of nature prevailed, and we all had to deal with it in our own ways—with a darkening cloud over you two, especially, as you began your individual journeys absent the family unit.

This book is to add clarity to your journey, still under way many years later, and to underline my admiration for you both. Chase, you teach me about truly pursuing your passion for music, regardless of economics, and the arduous pathways to reaching success in your own way. Logan, you've shown me that grit means not quitting at any time—even if others would give you license to. You're nearing the end of four hard-fought, successful years at college, and I couldn't be happier for or more proud of you. This book is for you.

To my new wife, Gina.

You believed in me when I didn't. You didn't care that I had millions of dollars in liabilities and a mountain of post-apocalyptic crevasses to bridge. You didn't care that your life as you knew it could be collateral damage. You believed in us and courageously stood strong next to me, holding me when I swayed, steadying me when I spun.

Even during the worst years of the divorce and financial hobbling, I would get up, fight all day, and then come back to my cloud of love and security with you.

I was most fortunate as I stood overlooking the Mediterranean, repeating vows to my new bride in Italian as we eloped, a wedding party of two.

To my parents, Tom and Ellie.

Strength by action. Resilience with commitment. Power through positivity. Greatness by example.

To the Well-Deserving Survival Cabinet of *Spinning into Control*

In the particularly lengthy "evaluation" stage of writing this book, I was truly touched by the willingness of so many dedicated readers of early drafts of the manuscript. Many were friends; others were just curious and altruistic acquaintances who showed an interest in me and the subject.

To my father and mother (Tom and Ellie Finley). My son Logan, who aspires to be a writer. My sister, Robin Arnold, an avid reader, and her daughter, my niece Thea Arnold, who combed through long and sometimes awkward prose to lend a hand in prioritization and encouragement.

To my dear and close friends who took many hours out of their busy schedules to read and comment extensively: Mario Sinicariello, Doug Bell, Dan Zelman, Keith Brown, Marty Erbaugh, Richard Seaman, Jim Hickey, Rick Doody, Eric Schreibman, Dr. Raj Aggarwal, Dr. Will Mandel, Luke Bishop, Steve McPeake, John Cregan, and John DiJulius . . . many with stories of their own to share.

To my curious coworkers and associates Mark Gregg, Wade Dougherty, and Meghan Vince; maybe they've discovered a new and perhaps humbler person than the one who they'd seen sitting behind the big desk in the back-corner office.

To my beloved Russian immigrant friends, all of whom I find so passionate and interesting, not to mention tenacious and hardworking. Many of you asked to stay anonymous; you know who you are. I learn from your outlook and enjoyment of freedom every day.

To my new friend, Dafna Kreimerman from Uruguay, who was visiting my office and showed significant interest in the subject. Your input was valued and incorporated.

To another new friend, Judith Cone, who I've worked with at the Burton D Morgan Foundation. Your enthusiastic feedback was "spot on."

To my treasured friends and true inspirations Wade Hoag

and his father Mike. I hang on your every word and appreciate your passion in contributing to this book.

To my friend who will regretfully never read this acknowledgment, Roger DePenti (Stefani Schaefer's husband, who you read about in chapter 1), who is physically with us and even smiles when we visit. I miss your kindness, your quiet strength, your sense of humor.

Of course, to my "adopted sister" Stefani Schaefer, and my "adopted niece" Siena and "nephew" Race. You've contributed so much, but your loss is deep. I'm so proud of you three. I will eagerly watch as each of you uses your overcoming of adversity to fuel your amazing accomplishments to come. To quote Dr. Seuss, "Oh, the places you'll go!"

Kelsey Grode and I worked together almost daily for nearly two years on every aspect of this book. She pursued survival stories I had earmarked during my own research and suggested other appropriate stories that fit the messages and philosophies I wanted to convey. Kelsey had incredible insights and a creative intellect that let the words and ideas flow freely. She is brilliant at her craft and is one who lives the REACH protocol in her everyday life. I'm proud of her and will miss our interaction and idea exchange.

Finally, to Gina. We celebrate seven years together, five of them as husband and wife. My appreciation for you broadens every day. You give everything and ask for nothing. You trust me implicitly; you love me with all your heart. You made me feel on top of the world while I was in total darkness. I will never forget.

ABOUT THE AUTHOR

Patrick T. Finley is founder and chairman of OMNI Property Companies—a conglomerate of commercial real estate companies and strategic partnerships. He has been involved as a real estate entrepreneur for more than thirty years, starting when he was working toward his degree in finance from the University of Akron. Simultaneously, he became the youngest person, at age eighteen, to ever obtain a Series 7 stock broker license from the Securities and Exchange Commission. Additionally, he obtained several student rental properties at the university, thereby starting what is now the Omni portfolio. After receiving his degree, Pat worked at various finance and real estate–related jobs while building Omni and partnering with fellow classmates to create Pride One, a residential and commercial real estate development business. He also received his Certified Commercial Investment Manager (CCIM) designation during this time. Today, his real estate consulting clients and partners include many well-known international publicly traded companies as well as locally owned and operated businesses.

Pat has been involved as a principal in more than $2 billion in real estate projects. In 1999, he was chosen as one of *Crain's Cleveland Business* magazines' "40 under 40." He was selected to be a member of the Leadership Cleveland Class of 2004. Pat has been chairman of the Cleveland chapter of Young Presidents Organization (YPO) and a member of the Entrepreneurs Organization (EO). He was named the NAIOP 2000 Developer of the Year and served as its president in 2004. Pat was recently the chairman of the board for North Coast Community Homes, a nonprofit housing organization serving approximately one thousand developmentally disabled residents. He serves as one of six trustees on the Burton D. Morgan Foundation, a $162 million grant-making foundation that focuses on entrepreneurial education.

Pat is an active jet airplane and helicopter pilot, scuba diver, snow and water skier, cyclist, snowboarder, boater, exercise enthusiast, martial artist, and accomplished mountain climber. He and his father successfully summited Mount Kilimanjaro in Africa, the world's tallest freestanding mountain, in June 2014, making his father (then seventy-nine) the oldest American to summit to date.

Pat is married to Gina Marie and has two adult children: Chase, 23, and Logan, 20. He and his family reside in Bentleyville, Ohio.

His favorite book is *Oh, the Places You'll Go* by Dr. Seuss because it has a strong message for 6-year-old children to 106-year-old adults.

His favorite movie is *Saving Private Ryan* because it exemplifies the human sacrifice for the freedom we all enjoy to this day.